Will My Child Be Ready For School?

ELAINE McEWAN

Will My Child Be Ready For School?

ELAINE M^cEWAN

LIFEJOURNEY
BOOKS

LifeJourney Books is an imprint of David C. Cook Publishing Co.
David C. Cook Publishing Co., Elgin, Illinois 60120
David C. Cook Publishing Co., Weston, Ontario

Cover design by Dawn Lauck
Edited by LoraBeth Norton
Production by Steve Johnson

WILL MY CHILD BE READY FOR SCHOOL?

First Printing, 1990
Printed in the United States of America
94 93 92 91 90 5 4 3 2 1

McEwan, Elaine K., 1941—
    Will My Child Be Ready for School?/Elaine McEwan
            p.   cm.
    Includes bibliographical references.
    ISBN 1-55513-832-2
    1. Education, Preschool—Parent participation.   I. Title.
LB1140.35.P37M37   1990
372.21—dc20   90-43591
                                                              CIP

PART I

What Every Parent Needs to Know

CHAPTER 1

SCHOOL SUCCESS: WHAT DOES IT MEAN?

What is school success? What are the major attributes and skill areas of a successful student?

CHAPTER 2

YOUR CHILD'S MIND: THE CASE FOR EARLY LEARNING

How can I translate the current research into practical guidelines for working with my children? Why is it important for me to be personally involved in my children's learning?

CHAPTER 3

HOW DOES LEARNING HAPPEN?

How can I talk to educators about learning? What does all of the jargon really mean?

CHAPTER 4

WHAT KIND OF EARLY LEARNING IS BEST?

Should I be teaching my children math and reading in the crib? Is it possible to overdo it?

PART II

What Every Parent Ought to Do

PART III

What Every Parent Is Afraid to Ask

*To Aunt Ruth and Uncle Mel,
who have always believed
in the mind of the child.*

Before You Begin

School is an activity that has consumed most of my life. Very few crisp autumns have *not* found me sharpening pristine pencils and putting my name on a fresh assignment book or daily calendar.

As a student, I was an eager learner—so eager that the teacher of my one-room school in rural Michigan encouraged my parents to find extra activities and hobbies for my energies. As a teacher, I was intrigued by how students learned and often woke early in the morning to worry about those who were not learning. As a parent, I was fascinated by each developmental milestone in my children's lives; learning was an integral part of every day.

Today, as an elementary school principal, I am responsible for the schooling of hundreds of children. My energy, enthusiasm, and fascination for learning have not flagged. Each September I find myself looking for new ways to make school an enjoyable and successful experience for children.

The shelves of Christian bookstores are filled with volumes (including my own *Superkid? Raising Balanced Children in a Superkid World)* telling you how, when, and why to parent effectively. But exactly *what* you should be doing with your children from birth to five or six to prepare them for school—an activity that will consume nearly two decades and influence their lives forever after—is a topic that has been largely ignored.

Many parents (including, unfortunately, many Christian parents) have not always appreciated the mind of the child or diligently set about maximizing their children's learning potential. But God entreats us to "Train a child in the way he should go, and when he is old he will not turn from it" (Proverbs 22:6). We commonly view this command as a reference to spiritual training, but I believe the words encompass all areas of human development, including the intellectual dimension. The most important lessons about learning are not taught in kindergarten, high school, or even graduate school. They are learned in the home, and the course of study is completed by the age of six.

This book is organized into three parts: What Every Parent Needs to Know, What Every Parent Ought to Do, and What Every Parent Is Afraid to Ask. Each part can be read independently, so pick and choose the chapters that apply to your situation.

As you read the book, my goals for you are these:

(1) that you will appreciate the minds of your children and their enormous potential for learning

(2) that you will realize the value of time spent with your children in learning activities

(3) that you will understand the most important things necessary for your children's success in school

(4) that you will not let a day pass by without taking time out for learning with your children, and

(5) that you will see your children's minds as gifts to be developed—not to fulfill your own ambitions or to glorify yourself, but to bring glory to God's name.

What
Every
Parent
Needs
to
Know

CHAPTER ONE

School Success: What Does It Mean?

IT IS A WARM SEPTEMBER DAY. The new school year is full of promise. New crayons, freshly sharpened pencils, and unblemished notebooks sit atop each desk. As I make my rounds through the building, welcoming back students and teachers for another year of learning, I reflect on what I see in each classroom.

Even in the kindergarten, some children noticeably stand out from their peers. I can pick out those students who will sail through the school year with confidence and ease. Their parents will eagerly attend the fall parent conference, confident that all the news will be good. Their report cards will carry glowing reports of cooperation, enthusiasm, curiosity, and success. They sit in the circle, faces upturned, attentive to the story the teacher is reading. They are already learning! They will be successful students.

In the sixth grade, I wave quietly to returning students. Their teacher is talking about assignment notebooks and homework. Some students have already organized their desks and are taking notes. Their eyes do not leave the teacher as she moves about the classroom, checking to see that each student understands. Their hands are eagerly raised to ask questions and give answers. These are the successful students.

Were these children preordained at birth to move through school halls and classrooms with ease and confidence? Is there a "school success gene" that programs some children to walk away with academic honors and dooms others to frustration and failure? I do not believe so. I believe that all children have the potential to be "stars" at school, but it doesn't just happen. Some students have been nurtured and encouraged from birth to view learning as an exciting adventure. They have been stimulated and motivated from their early months to ask interesting questions and solve difficult problems. These are ones we call "successful."

WHAT DOES A SUCCESSFUL STUDENT LOOK LIKE?

What characteristics describe these remarkable children? Motivation, organization, intelligence, creativity, curiosity, self-discipline, independence, confidence, perseverance, initiative, cooperation. The list goes on and on. . . . Any teacher could probably add a dozen more traits: successful students study for tests, listen attentively, follow the teacher's directions, care about what they do, ask questions when they don't understand, read voraciously in their spare time, pay attention in class, and complete their homework regularly. They want to find out about things they don't know, and they challenge their teachers to be prepared. They are able to sort out all of the information they take in, identify what is important, and remember it. Even when the task is dull and boring, they persevere and complete it, for they can look ahead and see the larger goal.

Of course, the characteristics and habits I've just named don't all exist in any one child. Our goal is not superhuman children, but children who fit most of these categories most of the time.

DO SUCCESSFUL STUDENTS JUST KNOW MORE?

Many reports critical of education lament how little our students actually know. E.D. Hirsch's book, *Cultural Literacy*, discusses this problem in depth. In a follow-up book, *The Dictionary of Cultural Literacy*, Hirsch sets forth the facts that all supposedly literate adults should know. As an educator, I find this approach more than a little worrisome.

Successful students don't just win at Trivial Pursuit; they know how to learn. They solve problems and put ideas together in new ways. They are able to predict what is coming next, whether it be the conclusion of a fairy tale or the questions on the final exam. Successful students are able to read with understanding and write with clarity and expression. They are usually just a step ahead of their fellow classmates and sometimes even their teacher.

But just what determines who will be successful in school and who will not?

WHAT IS THE BEST INDICATOR OF SCHOOL SUCCESS?

In the "business" of education, we principals and teachers have no control over our students' experiences before they come to school. We have to work hard to assure that all students are learning now. But twenty years ago Dr. Burton White, a Harvard researcher, noticed the same phenomenon I do each fall as I walk around my school: some students are more successful than others. White had plenty of time, as researchers often do, and wanted to know what had happened to these children, whom he labelled "competent," before they came to school. Perhaps if he found out what the "secret" was, he theorized, it could be shared and taught to all parents.

First he identified some abilities that characterized successful students. He found that these students:
- obtained and held the attention of adults in socially acceptable ways
- showed pride in personal accomplishment
- used resources effectively
- planned and carried out complicated activities
- could deal in abstract thinking
- were developing good language
- perceived discrepancies and small details
- engaged in make-believe
- led and followed peers.

Then he put the children into three categories—those who had superior, average, and below-average amounts of these academic and social abilities. When the home environments of these three groups were examined, some startling things were found.

Mothers of average students took a hands-off attitude about raising their children. They sat back and let things happen. The mothers of below-average students engaged in some very detrimental child-rearing practices, resulting in children who were substantially lower in intellectual competence, were least able to interact with adults, and exhibited more negative social behavior. The mothers of children with superior academic abilities, however, structured an environment that included the following:

- a variety of toys and learning experiences
- their own availability and approachability as a resource
- a child-proofed home that offered children the freedom to explore
- a running verbal commentary about everything that was happening
- appreciation and excitement for each new accomplishment.[1]

White's study demonstrated that what happens at home during the first five years of a child's life has a sizeable impact on intellectual development and thus on success in school. In Chapter 2 we will see how this research can be translated into practical suggestions for parents.

WHAT DOES THE BIBLE SAY ABOUT SCHOOL SUCCESS?

You've just read what one researcher says about the importance of parents. When we turn to the Bible, we find that God has also laid the responsibility of child rearing squarely on our shoulders.

"Train a child in the way he should go, and when he is old he will not turn from it" (Proverbs 22:6). As I pointed out in the foreword, this verse includes all areas of human development—intellectual, emotional, social, and physical as well as spiritual. School success is dependent on being well-rounded, but we cannot deny that the intellectual dimension plays a major role. The mind of a child is a precious gift from God, one which we are charged to develop to its fullest.

The story of the talents (Matthew 25) relates the harsh words Jesus has for those who do not use the gifts that God has given them. I believe God wants us to do the same with the talents and gifts of our children: nurture and develop them.

The early Puritans established schools to teach their children to read for one purpose—so they could read the Bible. They recognized that without literacy, the building of one's religious faith is severely inhibited. Without the ability to read, think, and communicate, our children will be cut off from learning about God's will and sharing their faith with others. Although the purposes of schooling are much broader in today's society, the abilities to read, write, and speak effectively are especially critical if we want our children to be effective Christians in today's complex world.

WHEN SHOULD I START THINKING ABOUT SCHOOL SUCCESS?

It may be difficult to visualize your bouncing bundle or terrific toddler in a first-grade classroom, much less in junior or senior high school. But now is the time to begin! To think about school readiness when your child is four or five may be a little late. The process begins when your baby opens his eyes and gazes into his mother's face after delivery. Your newborn is beginning to learn at that very moment.

You may feel a bit embarrassed about wanting bright children who do well in school. Parents will usually admit to wanting healthy children or happy children, but will seldom verbalize this secret desire to have successful students. Perhaps you feel that it is presumptuous at least, and sinful at worst, to desire that your children should be bright and do well in school. But don't be shy! There's nothing wrong with wanting your children to develop to their fullest potential.

Believe me, life will be easier if you raise successful students. You will rarely have to nag about homework. You won't have to offer money for good grades. You probably won't have to hire tutors or send your children to remedial summer school. Visits to school and parent-teacher conferences will be enjoyable experiences. Your child will be self-motivated and eager to learn.

What's wrong with wanting more time to enjoy and talk to your children instead of worrying and nagging about school? Nothing. Besides, God expects it. He wants us to nurture and challenge our children. He desires the best that we can offer.

WHERE DO I BEGIN?

Were you a successful student? Then your own child will have a much better chance of succeeding in school. You will no doubt repeat most of the positive parenting practices that you experienced in your own home setting. Unfortunately, the converse is also true. If school was difficult for you, then you will need to read this book with special care and commitment. For you, parenting a successful student will mean changing parenting patterns that were established long ago. You will need to pray for God's wisdom to establish a new set of parenting behaviors, behaviors that will set your child on the road to school success.

The most important place for all of us to begin is on our knees. We cannot do it alone; we need God's guidance each step of the way as we raise our children. God wants us to be successful parents. The same love, teaching, discipline, excitement, and care that He shows toward us is what He expects from us as parents. There is no better model than God the Heavenly Father.

In the chapters ahead, we'll discover what we as parents can do to create a home environment that encourages a love for learning and nurtures successful students.

1. White, Burton L., *Experience and Environment: Major Influences on the Development of the Young Child, Volume II*, Englewood Cliffs, New Jersey, Prentice Hall, Inc., 1978.

CHAPTER TWO

Your Child's Mind: The Case for Early Learning

IT'S A BIT SCARY BECOMING A PARENT. You have to worry about natural childbirth classes, ultrasound readings, fetal monitoring, educational toys, and custom-designed wallpaper to stimulate the development of brain cells. And the more you learn, the more intimidating the prospect becomes.

When Dick and I had our first baby back in 1970, things like daycare and "quality time" had yet to be discovered. We only had to pick out a boy's name and a girl's name and figure out how we were going to live on one income, for there was no thought of my continuing to work. As soon as I announced my pregnancy, my school superintendent promptly hired my replacement and sent me home to knit booties and blissfully await the arrival of our first child.

Blissfully, that is, until I got hold of Joan Beck's book *How to Raise a Brighter Child.* The book terrified me. I thought that babies popped out with all of their buttons preset. That's what I'd learned in my child development classes in college. Rousseau, Piaget, and Gesell all told us that children pass naturally through stages of development, and the best course of action for parents is to stand by and record the developments in our baby books. I thought that once we'd conceived and brought this child into the world, we only had to keep its stomach filled and its diapers dry. But now Joan Beck told me that I was also responsible for developing brain cells and nurturing cognitive development. What did I know about brain cells and cognition?

So I began to read, tackling this new area of knowledge as though I were preparing for a final exam. Most of the volumes I explored were written for academics, for the popular books on the topic would not appear for years to come. But the field was an exciting one. I became addicted to reading about the mind of the child. *Revolution in Learning; A Child's Mind; Studies in Cognitive Growth; Intelligence and Experience*—I sampled them all. Raising a child was going to be much more interesting and challenging than I had anticipated!

Our own personal research projects, Emily and Patrick, are now in college, but my enthusiasm for this topic continues unabated. Research on early learning has increased by geometric proportions, and the popular books on the subject now fill several shelves at the public library.

I'd like you to make room on those shelves for one more book, because I believe that every parent needs to catch my enthusiasm and interest in developing their children's intellectual potential to the fullest. In order to give your children the best learning environment you possibly can, you need to understand what psychologists, physicians, and educators have discovered during the past twenty-five years about the mind of the child.

IS A CHILD'S IQ PREDETERMINED BEFORE BIRTH?

The concept of IQ (intelligence quotient) was developed by French psychologist Alfred Binet in 1905. IQ is a numerical indicator of cognitive ability in three areas: verbal, non-verbal, and performance. Fifty years ago psychologists and physicians believed that IQ was unchangeable. Babies were born with a fixed ability; heredity was the sole determiner of intelligence.

But in the late fifties and early sixties, researchers began to pay more attention to evidence that suggested otherwise. For example, when identical twins were separated and raised in different environments, their IQs turned out to be quite different, suggesting that environment played an important role in developing ability.

Other evidence that seemed to conflict with the "immutable IQ theory" came from comparing children raised in orphanages to those from foster homes. Those raised in the more stimulating environment of foster homes nearly always had higher IQs than their counterparts reared in the sterile and deprived orphanage environments. Although the "immutable IQ theorists" tried to explain away the evidence, the research indicated that IQ was indeed changeable.

In 1961, Dr. J. McVicker Hunt, a pioneer researcher in the effect of environment on intelligence, wrote: "It appears that the counsel from experts on child-rearing during the third and much of the fourth decades of the twentieth century to let children be while they grow and to avoid excessive stimulation was highly unfortunate."[1] Today, scientists can show us how early learning actually changes the size and chemical functioning of the brain cells.

HOW MUCH IS IQ DETERMINED BY ENVIRONMENT?

Most research studies indicate that about seventy percent of an individual's IQ is attributable directly to genetics: nearly three-fourths of our intelligence is the result of who our parents happen to be. But that leaves over twenty-five percent attributable to other factors—over one-fourth of our child's intellectual potential will be affected by the kind of early learning environment we establish in our homes.

A recent French study of adopted children graphically shows how both environment and heredity impact a child's IQ. Thirty-eight children who had been adopted across socio-economic lines were compared. The researchers found that regardless of who the adoptive parents were, adopted children born to more intelligent parents had IQs averaging nearly twelve points higher than those of children born to less intelligent parents.

At the same time, children raised by families where educational and learning advantages were available had IQs averaging more than fifteen points higher than those who had been raised in less advantageous environments, regardless of the intelligence of their birth parents.

With that much of a child's potential "undetermined" at birth, we have a marvelous opportunity, yes, even responsibility, to make a positive impact on our children's intellectual development.

IS THERE A CRITICAL TIME FOR EARLY LEARNING?

Most new moms and dads send out photos of their offspring taken during the first few hours of birth. Anxious grandparents study these photos for glimpses of the child this infant will become. Does he look like my Aunt Mary or your great-grandfather Herman?

We are so often concerned with the physical aspects of the newborn that we forget he is a person, too. Even though hospitals are not yet providing parents with microscopic snapshots of the newborn's brain, researchers find such photographs extremely interesting. The photos show millions of brain cells not yet connected to one another or operative.

The most critical period for the development of these connections, or synapses, between the cells is the first three years of life. In fact, seventy to eighty percent of these connections are formed by the age of three. Of course, we know that the child of three does not have the emotional maturity or the reasoning capabilities of an adult, but much of the *potential* to learn, process information, and think is locked in place by that age.

Knowing that IQ is not predetermined at birth, and that environmental influences can affect its development, the next logical question is this: when should parents start thinking about their children's early learning?

Dr. Benjamin Bloom examined more than one thousand studies that measured intelligence of large groups of individuals at several critical checkpoints in their lives. He concluded that, with regard to academic achievement, at least one-third of the development at age eighteen took place prior to the child's entrance into first grade. "The child does not come to the first grade of school as a *tabula rasa* on which teachers will indelibly imprint the educational values and competencies prized by the culture. Quite the contrary, the child enters first grade after having gone through perhaps the most rapid period of development which will take place throughout his life." [2]

Don't confuse potential for learning or ability to learn with knowledge. Of course your children will acquire many skills and a great deal of knowledge during the school years. But, what children do bring to school from the home environment is the ability to learn. The greater this ability, the more children will get out of the school experience and the easier it will be for them.

ARE BABIES REALLY THAT SMART?

Although the brain of a newborn baby is filled with millions of unconnected synapses, connections start forming almost immediately after birth. That little bundle that seems only to eat, sleep, and cry is actually learning at a fantastic rate!

One of my children's favorite read-aloud stories was *Are You My Mother?* by P. D. Eastman. A baby bird falls out of the nest and tries to find his mother. Before he finds his way back to the nest, he asks the question "Are you my mother?" of a kitten, hen, cow, and even a steam shovel.

We used to think that newborns were a little like that baby bird, not able to recognize their own mother, much less do anything else. But experiments with infants less than twenty-four hours old demonstrate that newborns can:

- tell the difference between sweet and sour liquids and express a preference for the sweet
- distinguish patterns and express a preference for a new design
- tell what direction a sound is coming from and express a preference for some sounds over others
- differentiate smells
- respond to soothing and gentle human contact.[3]

Experienced and sensitive mothers and fathers are not surprised by these research results. Their common sense has always told them their baby was a person, too.

ARE THEY REACHING THEIR POTENTIAL?

Are we trying to produce geniuses? No. We are just trying to make sure that all children reach the potential that is within them. Heredity, of course, places an upper limit on our intelligence, but what we don't know is how high that ceiling is.

The story is told of a classroom teacher who was given her class list for the school year with numbers next to each name. She assumed that the numbers were IQ scores and taught her class accordingly. The numbers ranged from 128 to 148—a class of very gifted children, she thought. It was only in June, after a year of lively lessons, exciting experiments, and enriched field trips, that she discovered what the figures really were: locker assignments!

Her approach during the school year had been geared in just one direction—toward teaching gifted children. The children rose to meet her expectations and blossomed in the environment she provided. As parents, we should have the same set of expectations; our children are gifted, and our job is to bring out that giftedness.

JUST HOW IMPORTANT IS MOM (OR DAD)?

Next we will investigate some research studies that illustrate the importance of what happens in the home between the years of birth and five. Imagine the whole process as a journey. School is our first destination; life is the ultimate goal. We all need a road map for getting our children to these destinations. If explorers and adventurers have charted out the journey in advance, why shouldn't we take advantage of their knowledge and expertise?

Of course, each of our journeys will be slightly different. The weather, the seasons, and our mode of transportation will all have an effect. One child may be strong-willed and challenging; another of sunny temperament and malleable; a third child may be quiet and introspective. But regardless of your children's individual strengths and weaknesses, surely it makes sense to consult the map the researchers have provided before making decisions about how to take the trip.

IT'S WHAT YOU DO, NOT WHAT YOU ARE

In the early sixties, James Coleman issued a report stating that the best predictor of a child's success in school was the educational level of the mother.[4] That statement makes it sound like a child will succeed in school *solely* because of what the mother was.

But of course, it isn't what you are—it's what you *do*. It isn't where you live, how much money you make, which preschools you send your children to, what your level of education is, or even how many toys your children have, that determines whether their intellectual potential will be developed to the fullest. What you *do* is far more important than what you *are*. Keep that important idea in mind as you read on.

Maria Montessori, an Italian physician, put her beliefs about child development into practice with children from the slums of Rome in the early 1900s. Working at first with retarded children, she found her methods were so successful that her subjects outperformed normal children on school tests. Montessori consistently expressed a belief in the capacity of the young child to learn and the importance of the first five or six years of life long before this idea became a part of our conventional wisdom. Her practical approach to learning emphasized these concepts:

- Children learn through movement, and the best atmosphere for development is one in which they are unrestricted.
- Children learn through the exploration of their environment and need a variety of games, puzzles, and manipulatives to guide their progress to physical and mental independence.
- Children have an insatiable need to learn, and they gain a great deal of self-worth by learning to do things for themselves.
- Children learn best when they can make choices about what they want to do and the timetable by which to do them.[5]

Many early studies on the relationship between the home environment and school learning focused on race, social class, and educational background of the parents, all variables that can't be changed. One of the first studies to focus on what parents *do* rather than what they *are* took place in 1963. Researchers examined five different characteristics of the home environment: work habits of the family, academic guidance and support, stimulation in the home, language development, and academic aspirations and expectations.

When a combination of these factors was compared to a child's school achievement, the correlation was very high, regardless of where the child lived or how much money or education the parents had. Again, what parents did was clearly more important than what they were![6]

SO WHAT'S A MOM OR DAD TO DO?

Another investigation was made in 1966 by Dolores Durkin, who wanted to find out just what was going on in the homes of children who succeeded in school. She was especially interested in children who came to school already knowing how to read. Interviews with parents of these children uncovered four characteristics that all the homes had in common:

- Reading took place in the home. Parents read to children regularly. They themselves read. Reading was part of the family life-style.

- A wide range of printed materials was available in the home. Magazines, books of all kinds, and newspapers were on shelves and tables everywhere.

- Children had lots of contact with paper and pencil. (Perhaps in this modern age, our learners will have contact with computer terminals and word processors!) Children were able to produce their own scribbles and scrawls and do their own writing.

- Finally, all of the adults in the environment responded to what the child was trying to do. They took very seriously the child's attempts to make sense out of the written and spoken word.[7]

Dr. Burton White, director of the Harvard Preschool Project, had not yet published his landmark book *The First Three Years* when my children were born. But even though I hadn't read "the book," I had three advantages going for me as a mother. First, I had been blessed with wonderful parents. When all else fails, we parent as we have been parented. In the absence of a written plan, we fall back on what we know best.

Secondly, as an elementary school teacher, I had done a great deal of thinking about child development and had some specific goals in mind with regard to my children.

Lastly, I tapped all of the resources I could find—relatives, friends, and books—to find out more about this important topic. When I did read White's book, after my children were past their "first three years," his research validated for me what my common sense and heart had told me all along. White found that mothers of children who were successful in school did the following:

- child-proofed the home so children could have freedom to explore and discover
- provided an environment that was rich with toys and experiences
- acted as a resource for children by being available and approachable when questions or problems arose
- talked about everything they did
- shared the children's excitement with each new accomplishment.[8]

Now that you're thoroughly overwhelmed with what the research has to say, I'm going to try to boil it down for you into the most important principles. Although the ideas that follow are supported by research, I share them with you from my own personal experience. I've lived with each of these principles from birth to teen-age with my two children. I've watched their intellectual development and school success with wonder and delight. I know that these ideas work. The seven key areas are:

- language development
- reading aloud
- stimulating learning environment
- availability of toys and materials
- availability of mother (and father)
- academic aspirations and expectations
- modeling learning behavior

LANGUAGE DEVELOPMENT

Optimum language development is critical for a child's success in school, and the early years are an especially important time for acquiring language. In fact, young children are even able to learn more than one language with ease. I've recently acquired a tutor to help me learn Spanish. Her delightful daughter, Michelle, is bilingual at only two-and-a-half. She moves easily between speaking Spanish with her mom and English with me.

Children learn language in only one way—from listening to the people around them. The richer and more abundant the language they hear on a daily basis, the more well-developed their own language will be. Both mothers and fathers should talk to their young children constantly.

I've recently carried on a highly scientific research study—observing parents with their toddlers while lunching at McDonald's. Oh, it looks as though I'm reading my newspaper while consuming my cheeseburger and fries, but in reality I'm eavesdropping on conversations. I've noticed that some parents seldom speak a word to their children. Obviously these are caring mothers and fathers, since they've taken time out from their jobs or chores around the house to spend "quality time" with their children. But they aren't using their time in the best possible way when they stare vacantly into space or read a newspaper.

It may seem awkward at first to chatter with a child. You may feel that others are wondering how you can talk so animatedly with a toddler or preschooler. But forge ahead . . . keep talking! Stimulating the development of language in your children from birth to age five is one of the most important things you can do to put them on the road to success in school. You can enhance language development in the following ways:

- Talk to your children from birth even though the conversation may be one-sided. Never use baby talk.
- Talk out loud about what you are doing, seeing, or feeling whenever you have the chance. Explain everyday actions or name common objects.
- Use appropriate vocabulary, good grammar, and well-developed sentence structure.
- Use a pleasant tone of voice and inject humor and animation into your conversation.
- If a child speaks just one word, answer in a complete sentence with several new ideas added.
- Use praise and encouragement whenever possible.
- Sing hymns, choruses, or favorite songs to your child.
- Recite poetry, Bible verses, or nursery rhymes on a regular basis.
- Listen to your children as attentively as you would to adults. Show by your body language and facial expressions that you are interested in what they are saying.
- Play word games, rhyming games, guessing games—any kind of game that highlights the unique sounds of the language.
- Include your children in dinner-time conversations that revolve around discussions of what happened during the day. Even babies in high chairs can be made to feel a part of the family during this important time.

READING ALOUD AND READING RELATED ACTIVITIES

I consider reading to be the single most important habit that you can instill in your children. Reading aloud gives children an understanding of the purpose of the printed word and a growing familiarity with written language that is essential to a successful experience with reading in school. Reading aloud exposes children to an exciting world of information, imagination, and stimulation.

There are wonderful age-graded materials, both secular and Christian, from which to choose. Suggestions for what to read and how to get started on this activity can be found in a number of resources. Encouraging a love of reading and reading readiness skills can be done in the following ways:

- Read aloud to your children on a daily basis. During the early years, spend just a few minutes at a time. As your children grow older, increase the length of the read-aloud period.
- Provide a variety of books for your children to "read" on their own.
- Capture every opportunity for reading—street signs, grocery store displays, even cereal boxes.
- Visit the church library on a regular basis.
- Get a public library card and sign up for the weekly story hours when your children are old enough.
- Provide writing materials so your children can "write" their own stories.
- Read yourself, so that your children can see what an important part of your life reading is.

A PHYSICAL ENVIRONMENT THAT STIMULATES LEARNING

The table was not my favorite. Purchased when we were newlyweds, it seemed ugly and out of place when we moved to our new home. We planned to replace it immediately, but then realized that the children always gravitated to that table to fingerpaint, scribble with markers, and glue sequins on home-made Christmas ornaments. On more than one occasion I could be found with a scouring pad, cleaning Elmer's glue or fingerpaint from the formica surface. There was something about that table with its spacious and indestructible surface that caused the creative juices to flow, and whenever Dick and I talked of replacing it, a cry would go up from the children, "Where will we work?"

Not only did my children do their best work at that ugly table, but I managed to work my way through two advanced degrees typing papers there. We worked side by side, the children and I, interrupting each other when needed. When the children graduated to desks in their bedrooms, and I graduated to a computer in the family room, we felt able at last to let that table go.

Having a place where children can make messes, experiment with paints and markers, play games, and put giant puzzles together is far more important than any decorating scheme, and I'm not sorry we delayed our original plan for many years. Other things you should do to provide an environment that stimulates learning are:

- Child-proof your home so that you won't have to restrict your infant or toddler to a playpen, crib, or high chair.
- Encourage your children to explore, touch, and move about freely.
- Provide a place that is easily accessible where your children can store books, toys, and supplies. This will help them make choices about what to do in their play time and be responsible for caring for their toys.
- Don't worry about keeping things excessively neat. Creativity doesn't blossom in obsessive orderliness.

THE AVAILABILITY OF TOYS AND MATERIALS

We recently asked our children to discard some of their childhood playthings to make room for their growing collection of records and books. The dolls, teddy bears, blocks, and puzzles evoked nostalgia and amusement, but also several interesting observations.

I realized over the years that we had spent a sizable amount of money on playthings for our children. Had our investment been worthwhile? I asked myself. Looking at our teenagers, who are creative and intelligent human beings with varying abilities and interests, I felt no regret at having purchased a wide variety of toys and games that stimulated those interests and fostered those abilities.

Play is the work of the young child. The provision of toys and materials with which children can play is a key factor in their intellectual development. In addition to toys, there are many inexpensive materials that encourage creativity in children—paper, cardboard, yarn, spools, pots and pans, egg and milk cartons, discarded clothes, large and small boxes—and the list goes on and on.

Here are the most important things that you can do as you provide toys and materials for your child:

- Provide toys that are age-appropriate.
- Select toys that are safe.
- Choose toys that stimulate the creative development of your children. Stay away from an over-abundance of batteries, flashing lights, and voice synthesizers.
- Provide a rich sampling of art and craft materials that are appropriate for your children's ages.
- Don't worry about how your children play with toys. Just provide the resources and let them do the rest.

THE AVAILABILITY OF A MOTHER (OR FATHER)

The presence of a full-time mother, father, or other committed care-giver for a child during the crucial years from birth to three or beyond is the fifth important ingredient in creating an intellectually stimulating environment. Burton White recommends that a mother or other caregiver spend at least half her children's waking hours available to them, but never hovering over them. The children should not concentrate their energies solely on that person. White's other recommendations for being available include:

- Stop to help with a problem whenever children indicate a need for help, and take time to explain your solution.
- Respond as promptly and as often as possible to your children.
- Make an effort to understand what your children are doing and saying.

- Don't make all of your children's play decisions for them. Permit them to make most of the decisions about where and how to play.[9]

ACADEMIC ASPIRATIONS AND EXPECTATIONS

As parents we are constantly communicating our expectations to our children. We expect them to brush their teeth each night; we expect them to share their toys and be kind to friends; we expect them to say thank you when someone gives them a gift. Even though they may not always do what we expect, we nevertheless keep communicating these most important messages.

We need to communicate the same messages with regard to our academic aspirations and expectations. You probably won't be telling your toddler about your expectations that he'll attend college or be an engineer, but you'll surely be talking about how much fun he'll have in school when he goes or how you want him to do the best possible job in coloring the picture to send to Grandma.

In a study of 120 immensely talented individuals, a common thread was discovered running through each family. "The parents' commitment to the productive use of time and doing one's best was evident in the values they taught their children. The parents expected all family members to learn this code of conduct, and the models the parents provided of working hard and setting high standards of performance were clearly recognized by the children."[10]

The same thread of academic expectation was discovered by Victor and Mildred Goertzel when they studied the biographies of 400 famous twentieth century men and women: "In almost all the homes there was a love for learning in one or both parents, often accompanied by a physical exuberance and a persistent drive toward goals. Fewer than ten per cent of the parents failed to show a strong love for learning."[11]

I believe that parents must have their own agenda of goals to accomplish if children are to understand the importance of study and learning. I've seen many a brand-new mom who spent all of her waking hours playing with her child. She decided which toys to use for playtime. She decided how to play with the toys. She decided when the playtime was over.

I'm not suggesting that parents shouldn't engage in play with their children. There will be many suggestions in the chapters to follow for just that. What I am suggesting is that children need to see the accomplishment of tasks as an important aspect of grown-up life. They need to know that their job is to play and that mother (or father's job) is sewing, mowing, cooking, fixing, building, reading, writing, or whatever the project may be. You can communicate these same expectations in a variety of ways:

- Praise your children for their accomplishments.
- Talk about the future and what it holds in terms of schooling.
- Provide support and help if your children are having difficulty in reaching goals they have set for themselves.
- Talk with your children about jobs that people do and the kinds of education and training they need to be successful.
- Show your children that reading and writing are important to you and tell them that you know they will learn to read and write well also. Demonstrate these skills for your child and emphasize how important they are to success in school as well as success in life.
- Communicate to your children that "if it's worth doing, it's worth doing well."

MODELING LEARNING BEHAVIOR

Four-year-old Emily gathered the Webster's dictionary, *Bartlett's Familiar Quotations*, the enormous family Bible, and several other "big books." She arranged them on the table, put a fresh sheet of paper in the typewriter, and announced, "I'm going to study." The process had taken nearly half an hour. Somewhere—no doubt from her parents or baby-sitters—Emily had picked up the idea that if you wanted to study, you gathered big books, fresh paper, and a typewriter around you.

Modeling a learning life-style is the last of the seven areas in which parents must excel if they want their children to be successful in school. Modeling this life-style is more than just reading in front of your children. You should also:

- Develop routines and schedules in your home so children know what your priorities are.
- Tackle a new skill or field of knowledge and let your children see that learning is fun.
- Work on projects that require the reading of directions for completion (home remodeling, gardening, crafts, cooking).
- Look up words you don't know in the dictionary.
- Look up answers to questions you don't know in books or encyclopedias.
- When your children ask a question that you can't answer, find a book that does and read it together.
- Accomplish something worthwhile each day toward the achievement of a goal.

WILL MY CHILDREN SUCCEED IF I DON'T DO IT ALL?

But of course. No one is keeping track of the times we fail, thank goodness. There are no perfect parents, just as there are no perfect kids. There are days that we don't read aloud. There are days when if Johnny interrupts you one more time while you're trying to finish making dinner, you'll put him in solitary confinement for the rest of his life. There are days when you just want to escape from the dreariness and tedium of being a parent.

But on the good days—those days when the sun is shining and we're proud to be parents—on those days we want to know exactly what we ought to be doing and aspire to be doing the best. Those are the days that we will talk with our children, be available when they need our help, encourage and support them—even if it means answering the same question for the fiftieth time.

Since we're obligated for twenty-four hours a day until they leave for college anyhow, why not do everything we can to increase the likelihood that our children will develop to their full potential and achieve school success?

1. Hunt, J. McVicker. *Intelligence and Experience*. The Ronald Press, New York, 1961, p. 362.

2. Capron, Christiane and Michel Duyme. *Nature*. August, 1989.

3. Bloom, Benjamin. *All Our Children Learning*. McGraw-Hill Book Co., New York, 1981, p. 72.

4. Beck, Joan. *Best Beginnings*. G.P. Putnam's and Sons, New York, 1983, p. 108.

5. Coleman, James and others. *Report on Educational Opportunity in the United States*. Washington, D.C.; U.S. Government Printing Office, 1966.

6. Montessori, Maria. *The Absorbent Mind*. Holt, New York, 1967.

7. Bloom, op. cit., pp. 94-101.

8. Durkin, Dolores. *Children Who Read Early*. Teachers College Press, New York, 1966.

9. White, Burton L. *The First Three Years of Life*. Prentice-Hall, Inc., Englewood Cliffs, New Jersey, 1975.

10. Bloom, Benjamin, Editor. *Developing Talent in Young People*. Ballantine Books, New York, 1985, p. 441.

11. Goertzel, Victor and Mildred G. Goertzel. *Cradles of Eminence*. Little, Brown and Company, Boston, 1962, p. 272.

CHAPTER THREE

How Does Learning Happen?

IN THE FALL OF 1983 I WAS A BRAND-NEW SCHOOL PRINCIPAL. Armed with my sheepskin and dressed for success in a navy suit and bow tie, I was ready to change the world. One of the first meetings I attended included the school psychologist, the learning disabilities teacher, and the Talbots, parents of a fourth grader. I was merely an observer as the professionals shared the results of the testing they had given Ronnie.

The learning disabilities teacher spoke first. She talked about achievement and ability differentials and how we might program for differences in learning styles. The psychologist followed with a dissertation on sequential and simultaneous processing that included a brief discourse on auditory and visual discrimination. She concluded by asking if there were any questions.

I stole a sideways glance at the parents. They had been listening attentively and, amazingly enough, they had no questions. Perhaps they knew more than I did. I suspected, however, that their silence, like mine, had little to do with understanding. We were just too baffled by the jargon.

That day I began my crash course in "learning about learning." Only if I knew what all the terms meant could I translate them into meaningful explanations to parents. What happens when kids learn? What's the difference between verbal and non-verbal performance? How can I decide what my child's learning style is?

WHAT IS LEARNING?

I've spent hours poring through books trying to figure out the best way to help you understand what happens when we learn. So many writers, researchers, and theorists are offering information that, for the lay person, understanding the big picture can be very difficult. I've organized the information into a four-step process to help you. Remember, our goal is not to be experts, but to understand what is happening in the minds of our children.

In Step One of the process, input from the learning environment enters the brain through the senses. Some individuals learn better through one sense than through another. If you can remember ideas and information better through sight, you are called a visual learner, through hearing, an auditory learner.

Let's pretend that in Step One our imaginary learner has just touched a hot stove. He has taken in some very startling information through his sense of touch. The information has been relayed to his brain.

In Step Two, the wheels are beginning to turn. The brain is processing the input. Some individuals process sequentially and some process simultaneously. This may be accounted for by whether the processing is happening in the left or right hemisphere of the brain. But the majority of tasks are processed bilaterally, using both sides of the brain. We describe what is happening in the brain during this step as thinking, processing, or reasoning. Many messages are going through our imaginary learner's brain. "That hurt my hand." "Mommy said no." "Mommy slapped my hand." "Mommy got very excited when I did that."

In Step Three, learning is taking place in a variety of skill areas and on a variety of difficulty levels. These skill areas are particularly well defined for young children: motor, perceptual, language, conceptual, and cognitive. Learning can also be going on at a variety of different difficulty levels:

knowledge, comprehension, application, analysis, synthesis, and evaluation.

We are hopeful that our young learner is discovering that it is not a good idea to touch a hot stove. Perhaps if he has prior learning about "hot" things (bath water, hot chocolate, iron, curling iron), he is formulating the concept of what hot means. He is also learning what happens when he does something that displeases his mother. She says no. She raises her voice. She may even have slapped his hand in her distress over a possible injury to her child.

The more information that was given to the child in conjunction with his discipline, the more likely he will be to apply his knowledge the next time he is confronted with a hot stove. A critical skill that is needed at this point in our learning process is memory. Without memory, we would have to constantly relearn everything. There are occasions when we think our children have minds like sieves, but many concepts and skills need hundreds of repetitions in order to be remembered automatically.

The final step in the learning process is the output of the brain, its capacity or ability to do its job. This is called intelligence. According to some theorists, intelligence is multifaceted. In adults, intelligence is sometimes described as common sense or wisdom. Some aspects of intelligence are based on abilities in the area of language, and other aspects are based on non-verbal skills.

Do Children Learn Differently Than Adults?

The Swiss psychologist Piaget was a pioneer in studying how children learn. He spent thousands of hours observing his three children and keeping detailed notes on how they learned. Piaget theorized that there are distinct stages of development in a child's thinking and that children must pass through one stage before reaching the next.

His experiments demonstrated that a child's reasoning abilities are not developed enough before one year of age to determine that if an object is hidden, it has not ceased to exist. He showed that up until about the age of six, a child has a difficult time believing that a given quantity of milk or juice remains the same even though the size or shape of the container into which it is poured is changed. Piaget hypothesized that at about the age of seven, a child enters the third stage of development and seems to acquire fairly logical thinking capabilities. But not until the fourth stage, around the age of fourteen, can he deal with abstract ideas.

For many years, Piaget's theories affected beliefs about how children learn. But current research is showing this stairstep approach to learning to be too simplistic. Psychologists are finding that children are capable of mastering more complex tasks than we previously thought, particularly when they have good role models or are taught specific strategies.

WHAT ARE THE BASIC LEARNING STYLES?

Suppose that someone told you your life depended on mastering seven principles of survival in the wilderness. At the end of the course, you will be sent into the wilderness to survive. The choice of how you want to learn the seven principles is up to you. Would you prefer a lecture on the subject? Then you're probably an auditory learner. Perhaps you'd rather read a textbook. Visual learners need to see what they have to learn in print. Or would you choose to have an expert demonstrate each principle and then let you experience them for yourself? Then you're a kinesthetic learner.

I personally would like to read the material first, then attend the lecture, and finally try out what I've learned in the real world. The method you choose is probably closely related to your personal learning style, but each of us should become adept at getting input through all of our senses. In fact, that is why providing a wide variety of sensori-motor experiences is particularly important for children. We want them to become multi-sensory learners. Ideally, they should have the same opportunity to learn using all of their senses.

RIGHT-BRAINED, LEFT-BRAINED, OR SCATTER-BRAINED?

The discovery that the brain was divided into two sections or hemispheres resulted from work with "split-brain" patients, those who had the *corpus callosum* (the major connection between the hemispheres) cut due to severe epilepsy. Scientists discovered that certain behaviors and ways of thinking seemed to be centered in one hemisphere or the other.

Of course, unless our hemispheres have been disconnected, we all use both. But many individuals show a definite preference for either the right or the left side; thus the labels "right-brained" and "left-brained."

Distinctly right-brained individuals make better artists and performers. Distinctly left-brained people do better as accountants or chemists. We survived for centuries without knowing about hemisphericity, but an understanding of which thinking or reasoning patterns characterize each hemisphere, along with the related school skills, can be helpful for the parent.

Primarily left-brained individuals do their processing (thinking, reasoning) in an *analytical-sequential* fashion. They prefer verbal explanations, use language to remember, produce ideas logically, like structured experiences, and approach problems seriously.[1] The school skills that relate to this type of processing are: symbols, language, reading, phonics, locating details and facts, talking and reciting, following directions, listening, and auditory association.[2]

Individuals who are primarily right-brained do their processing in a *wholistic-simultaneous* way. They prefer visual explanations, use images to remember, produce ideas intuitively, prefer abstract thinking tasks, like open fluid experiences, and approach problems playfully.[3] The school skills that relate to this type of processing are: spatial relationships, mathematical concepts, color sensitivity, singing and music, art expression, creativity, and visualization.[4]

You have probably already drawn the conclusion that to succeed in school, a child's left brain needs to be well-developed. But just because an individual has a strong preference or strength in one hemisphere does not mean that development cannot take place in the other, particularly in the important years before school begins.

If I had known about hemisphericity back when Emily was growing up, I could have pegged her as a child with a strong right-brained orientation. Color was extremely important to her, and she had strong opinions about many of the serigraphs and oil paintings her father and I had collected. She went from drawing designs in marker on her white lamp shades at three to creating original T-shirts and award-winning ink drawings in high school.

Although we nurtured Emily's creativity and provided lots of arts and crafts materials, we also made sure that there were many verbal activities to balance the visual. In the developing child, it is important to provide activities and experiences that will help to develop the brain as a whole.

Don't get side-tracked on figuring out whether your child is left-brained or right-brained. Although it is fun to read about hemisphericity, unless half of the brain has been removed, we use the whole thing in an interactive way anyway!

SKILL AREAS FOR SCHOOL SUCCESS

There are five skill areas in which children need well-rounded development in order to achieve school success: motor skills, perceptual skills, language skills, conceptual skills, and cognitive skills.[5] In Chapters 6, 7, and 8, many activities will be suggested that enhance development in these five areas. For now, a simple description of each will suffice.

Motor development takes place when your child is free to move about and explore on her own. Confining a child to a playpen or crib for extended periods of time inhibits her motor development and keeps her from getting all of the touching, manipulating, pushing, pulling, and experimenting that she needs. Sub-skills that are a part of motor development include the ability to determine left and right, knowledge of body parts, eye-hand coordination, and balance.

Perceptual development, the second skill area, is the ability to see differences and likenesses in shape, line, size, and position. Visual discrimination, spatial perception, whole-part concepts, classification and grouping, and visual memory are all perceptual skills your child will need, especially for learning to read.

We have already mentioned *language development* in several other references. The more language experiences you provide for your child, the richer her background and readiness for school success will be.

Concept development, another important skill area, is very complex. The teaching of concepts takes time and a rich experience base. A child can only understand the concept of "animal" after reading lots of picture books, visiting a zoo or farm, petting the neighbor's dog, watching a National Geographic special on television, eating animal crackers, and asking hundreds of questions about what she has seen. Simply telling or giving a verbal definition is not enough for concept formation to take place. Many multi-sensory experiences must take place over a long period of time.

Cognitive development is what happens with all of the information children take in from their environment. Observing the details of life—the sights, sounds, and smells of a child's environment—is part of cognitive development. Comparing ideas and information and classifying them into categories is also cognitive development. Interpreting, describing, attending, creating—all are cognitive skills that are critical to school success.

DEVELOPING HIGHER-LEVEL THINKING SKILLS

Benjamin Bloom, a prolific writer and seminal thinker in the field of educational psychology, has given us one of the most helpful tools for understanding the different levels of thinking (reasoning, learning) that go on in our brains and in those of our young children. Called "Bloom's Taxonomy of the Cognitive Domain," this model can help you ask questions and structure learning activities that stretch your child's mind to higher levels.[6]

There are six levels: Knowledge, Comprehension, Application, Analysis, Synthesis, and Evaluation. Once you read the definitions, you will immediately recognize how you function on all of these levels every day.

At the *knowledge level* we are simply recalling facts and taking in information. Many adults mistakenly assume that when children can give back facts, they are bright. Knowledge is important, but what we do with those facts is even more important.

In the second level of the taxonomy, *comprehension*, we are beginning to understand what the facts mean. It is nice to know that $2 \times 2 = 4$, but comprehension means that not only do we know the multiplication facts but we can understand the concept of multiplication as a means of addition and can also figure out what 2×3 or 2×5 equals.

Application is the third level. Here the child can use the information and apply it in a real-life situation. If you were at the store and bought two suckers for twenty cents each, how would you figure out the total cost?

The next three levels, *analysis*, *synthesis*, and *evaluation*, are generally called the "higher-level" thinking skills. Many schools purposefully build questions and activities into their curricula to develop these skills. You can do the same with your preschooler on a more limited basis.

Analysis requires categorizing, filling-in, and analyzing similarities and differences. This activity can happen quite naturally when you're reading stories, depending on the age of the child. Which of the three pigs was the smartest? Why? Why do you think Frog and Toad like each other so much?

At the *synthesis* level, the child creates something brand new. Perhaps she'll draw a picture of a new idea she has. Perhaps she'll try to build a boat for Frog and Toad to sail away in. Perhaps she'll retell the story using puppets.

Evaluation, the highest level, calls upon the child to make judgments about something for which there is no right answer. That sounds like being a parent, doesn't it?

Using the different levels of thinking to ask questions or plan activities for your children can tax your own higher-level thinking skills. Don't be discouraged if the children don't respond. They may not be ready for the level. Try again some other day. Above all, don't jump to the conclusion that your children don't have any higher-level skills. They may not be ready or willing to demonstrate them to you.

CAN I HELP MY CHILDREN IMPROVE THEIR MEMORY?

The act of remembering is a critical aspect of learning. Who among us hasn't had a moment of panic when we've temporarily forgotten a well-used telephone number, or can't remember where we put that critical tax information?

There are three kinds of memory—sensory, for smells, touches, or sights; motor-skill memory, for physical activities like riding a bicycle; and verbal memory, for all the things we have heard, read, or thought. There are two kinds of verbal memory, short-term, for those items we only want to remember for a few seconds or minutes; and long-term, for the information and ideas we need to function as well-rounded human beings.

"During a lifetime the average person's memory can store billions of items, including 50,000 words and an even larger file of pictures—faces, scenes, and objects."[7] Educators are just beginning to realize that along with teaching facts and ideas, they need to teach strategies to help students remember key ideas and concepts.

WHAT ARE THE KEY FACETS OF INTELLIGENCE?

David Wechsler, developer of a widely used intelligence test, defined intelligence as "the global capacity of an individual to act purposefully, to think rationally, and to deal effectively with his environment."

Lewis Terman, whose studies of gifted children are still widely read today, cautioned against such a narrow view. "We must guard against defining intelligence solely in terms of ability to pass the tests of a given intelligence scale. It should go without saying that no existing scale is capable of adequately measuring the ability to deal with all possible kind of material on all intelligence levels."[8]

Terman's view of intelligence as being much broader than what can be measured on an intelligence test is supported by Howard Gardner, a Harvard psychologist. Gardner hypothesizes seven kinds of intelligence located in different parts of the brain: linguistic, logical-mathematical, spatial, musical, bodily kinesthetic, interpersonal, and intrapersonal. His ideas are fascinating and give us one more way to look at how to encourage the gifts and talents of our children.

There is much to be said for the self-fulfilling prophecy, however, so be careful not to type-cast your children on the basis of a few observations or less than expert judgments. When we were first married, my husband assured me that he was not mechanical. He'd been told by his parents that his older brother was the mechanical one, and therefore he had never explored or expanded that aspect of his talents. One day, after listening to him bitterly complaining about the charges at our local garage, I challenged him to replace the water pump on our automobile. That was the beginning of a new career in fixing things. Suddenly he discovered that he had mechanical ability after all.

If you promise not to start putting everyone you know, including your own children, into these categories, I'll explain them. For a more detailed discussion see *Frames of Mind: The Theory of Multiple Intelligences* by Howard Gardner.[9]

Linguistic intelligence is centered in language. Readers, writers, story-tellers are all linguistically gifted. Children with these gifts like to write, read, spell, do crossword puzzles, and play word games. (But all children should do these things as part of their growing up experience—not just those who seem to gravitate in that direction.)

Individuals with *logical-mathematical* intelligence think conceptually. They love figuring out the answers to difficult problems and most likely are very logical thinkers. Children with strengths in this area like computers, chess, checkers, strategy games, and puzzles.

Spatially intelligent people think in images and pictures. They can draw, design, and visualize the way a room will look with new furniture and wallpaper. Children with strengths in this area spend a lot of time in art-related activities.

Musical intelligence and *bodily-kinesthetic* intelligence relate to expertise in the areas of performing and composing music and sports and physical activities.

The last two areas are the most fascinating to me, since Gardner hypothesizes two areas that we frequently overlook when talking about intelligence: interpersonal and intrapersonal skills. The *interpersonal* people understand others. They are the leaders and communicators. The salesman that sold you the car you didn't think you needed probably had a high level of interpersonal intelligence.

Intrapersonal intelligence is just the opposite. Individuals with this quality are very independent. They rely on their own judgment, have a deep sense of self confidence, and generally don't care what everyone else is wearing or doing. They have their own agenda.

NOW THAT I KNOW IT, WHAT DO I DO WITH IT?

After reading this chapter, you may be wondering, "Am I supposed to do anything with this information? Will knowing how learning takes place change the way I function as a parent?"

Probably not. However, understanding what is happening as your children learn should help you as we launch into a discussion of the practical aspects of creating a learning environment in your home. More importantly, this understanding should give you a new appreciation for God's creation. The human mind and how it learns is miraculous. Understanding the multitude of ways that God uses the talents and gifts of His creatures is spectacular. Ask God to guide you as you nurture your children through their critical preschool years.

1. Webb, James T., Elizabeth A. Meckstroth., and Stephanie Tolan. *Guiding the Gifted Child.* Ohio Psychology Publishing Company, Columbus, OH, 1982, p. 52.
2. Vitale, Barbara Meister. *Unicorns are Real: A Right Brained Approach to Learning.* Jalmar Press, Rolling Hills Estates, CA, 1982, p.9.
3. Webb, op. cit.
4. Vitale, op. cit.

5. Smith, Helen Wheeler. *Survival Handbook for Preschool Mothers*, Follett Publishing Company, Chicago, 1977, pp. 101-120.
6. Bloom, Benjamin. *Bloom's Taxonomy of Educational Objectives, Book 1, Cognitive Domain*, New York, Longman, 1954.
7. Edson, Lee. *How We Learn*. Time-Life Books, New York, 1975, p. 84.
8. Webb, op. cit., p. 44.
9. Gardner, Howard, *Frames of Mind: The Theory of Multiple Intelligences*, New York, Basic Books, Inc., Publishers, 1983.

CHAPTER FOUR

What Kind of Early Learning Is Best?

As a trained teacher, I felt guilty that I wasn't teaching my toddler to read. Then I read a feature in the Chicago *Tribune* that promised parents they could easily teach phonics and have their children reading in a matter of weeks. I promised myself we would begin the following Monday.

The comic strip format made it all seem so simple. After all, I knew how to follow a lesson plan. I'd done it for seven years as a classroom teacher. So I set aside a quiet time when Patrick was napping, and my daughter and I sat on the couch to learn the letter names and sounds.

Emily was not at all impressed with the lesson content or my delivery. She refused to participate. She wanted to play with her toys and "read" on her own. The comic strip's author had not accounted for my strong-willed and obstinate child. Nor had she accounted for my frustration at not achieving success in the first twenty-four hours. Emily was definitely not in the mood for learning, and I was no longer in the mood for teaching.

Although I kept reassuring myself that she would learn to read one day, there continued to be nagging doubts. Perhaps other children would learn faster and have a head start. Until Emily came home from kindergarten one day in October and announced that she had learned to read that day, I continued to wonder if I had failed. But Emily learned to read in her own way and on her own timetable. My only failure as a parent had been to doubt my own good judgment in throwing the phonics lessons into the garbage.

The point of my story is this: there is a big difference between establishing an environment for learning in your home and "teaching your children" what you think they need to know based on some artificial timetable or list of developmental milestones. Children are funny about learning. They enjoy it, even hunger for it. But their efforts shouldn't be thwarted by pressure, competition, fear, or extrinsic rewards.

Children have an inborn need to explore, discover, and create. They will examine, manipulate, and investigate in a tireless fashion until they can make sense of their world—but only when they feel like it. Just try to impose *your* sense of priorities on a child, and learning will vanish like the sun behind a cloud.

THE DIFFERENCE BETWEEN TEACHING AND LEARNING

Teaching is defined by Webster as "giving instruction or lessons to a pupil or class." Learning is "the acquiring of knowledge or skill." The two are not necessarily related.

Teaching frequently takes place without learning, more often than most educators would like to admit. And, most assuredly, learning can take place without teaching. In fact, the best learning takes place when children experience and learn for themselves.

The kind of learning that prepares your child for success in school should not be characterized by formal lessons, programmed workbooks, flash cards, cassette tapes, or even step-by-step activities that fill the daily calendar in a rigid fashion. There are many curricula that promise instant results in basic skill areas. If you are teaching children of seven or eight, these may be quite appropriate. But for the infant, toddler, or preschooler, the curriculum should be centered around imaginative play and learning activities that capture the spontaneity of the moment, along with just plain exploration and fun.

Perhaps this low-keyed approach makes you nervous, after all you've read about the potential of the young child for learning. Just remember—the learning has to be the right kind!

The kind of learning we're talking about takes time . . . five or six years of time. Time of parent and child working side by side on complicated puzzles. Time of parent and child reading their favorite stories together. Thousands of mundane conversations while cooking dinner and driving to the hardware store. Millions of questions about why the sky is blue and where people go when they die. Minutes stolen here and there from housekeeping and chores to help a child solve a problem or just touch base with mother or father. These activities are the raw material of school success.

SEDUCTIVE PROMISES

There are many books on the market that promise instant results. They are seductive in their claims, and the stories they tell of two year olds who are doing Euclidean geometry are enough to give even the most conscientious parent a good case of the guilties.

Titles like *Teach Your Child to Read in 60 Days*, *Teach Your Baby Math*, and *How to Teach Your Baby to Read* are best-sellers. But their basic premises fly in the face of what we know about children and learning. Teaching "bits" of knowledge or isolated skills out of context does not "multiply" a child's intelligence. These approaches only serve to frustrate both parent and child.

MY CHILD VS. THE DEVELOPMENTAL CHARTS

Our pediatrician's office was beautifully decorated. Each examining room was papered with a different decor, designed to capture the attention of apprehensive parents and children. But the first thing that always caught my eye when we entered any of the examining rooms was the height and weight chart on the back of the door.

Does the same thing happen to you? New mothers always talk about how much weight their babies are gaining. In retrospect, it seems so silly, but we desperately want our children to be normal, if not outstanding—even if it's only in height and weight! There are many books that provide you with charts showing what your child should be doing at any given time. These charts only serve to make us feel anxious, and anxious is the last thing we need to feel.

The guidelines set forth in Chapter 2 never mentioned testing your children to see where they are in comparison to their peers. Those guidelines never mentioned enrolling them in special classes to make sure they turn somersaults before the chart says they should. Those guidelines said nothing about "teaching" your children anything; as a matter of fact, they distinctly avoided the use of the word "teaching" at all. They emphasized, rather, providing an environment that stimulates learning.

IS IT NORMAL TO WORRY AND FEEL GUILTY?

Everybody worries once in awhile. But sometimes the guilties attack us for days on end, especially if we spend time reading books like this one that tell you everything you "ought" to be doing! Even the author of this book didn't do it all, but that doesn't stop me from telling you just what you should do!

With two successful college students, I can now glibly give advice about "how to do it." But believe me, when I was going through it, I had more than my share of doubts and fears. I hope I can convince you, on the other hand, to relax, have fun, and enjoy!

WON'T MY CHILDREN BECOME ONE-DIMENSIONAL?

Many of the positive parenting behaviors that lead to intellectual development foster development in other areas as well. Emotionally well-developed children have a healthy level of self-esteem, self-motivation, independence, confidence, ability to handle new situations, ability to handle frustration, and a sense of accountability and responsibility. All of these characteristics will be fostered through their growing ability to master the world around them through learning.

Bright children generally have high levels of all of the characteristics just listed. The same is true of the social dimension. People used to think that bright kids were social misfits, but that is definitely not the case. Bright children have more hobbies and outside interests. They belong to more clubs and organizations. They are enthusiastic and involved in life. Bright youngsters are frequently more introspective and thoughtful about spiritual matters. They can read God's Word with understanding. They are able to see the relevance of the Scripture in their own lives more easily.

Because this entire book is devoted to the intellectual development of your children, I'm not suggesting that every other dimension be ignored. What I am suggesting is that maximizing your children's intellectual potential will have far-reaching benefits in every other dimension of their lives as well.

WHAT HAPPENED TO MOTIVATION, CREATIVITY, AND CURIOSITY?

In Chapter 1, I listed a number of qualities that characterize a successful student, but we've only discussed intellectual development. The omission of the others has been by design, not by accident. My own experience has shown that the home learning environment that promotes intellectual development has some wonderful side effects. It also results in the development of all of the other characteristics found in the successful student.

Rarely, if ever, have I had to nag my kids to complete assignments or work on special projects. Oh, there have been a few late nights when I was rushing to the library to find one last book for a report or prowling the supermarket aisles to find the precise shade of blue marker to color in the Pacific Ocean. But for the most part, my children have been responsible for what happens in their school life.

The minute they entered the formal school setting, I did not assume responsibility for their learning—they did. I always knew what was going on. We talked about their assignments, classes, and teachers. I volunteered my help whenever it was needed. I carpooled children to meet in project groups. I bought whatever supplies were needed to finish the diorama. But I didn't take responsibility for what happened at school, because I had no control over it. My children were responsible for their behavior and their performance.

I believe that motivation, creativity, perseverance, and all the other qualities that characterize a successful student will emerge as a natural by-product as children discover the joy of learning. You won't need to worry about motivating a student who loves to learn.

IS IT POSSIBLE TO OVERDO IT?

If your life is consumed with only one goal—raising your child's IQ—then you're definitely overdoing it. David Elkind, professor of child development at Tufts University, thinks parents of the eighties are overdoing it in a big way. In *The Hurried Child: Growing Up Too Fast, Too Soon* and *Miseducation: Preschoolers At Risk*, he is highly critical of parents who start children in formal academic settings too early.

Elkind points out that in Denmark, where reading instruction follows a language experience approach and formal instruction is delayed until age seven, there is almost no illiteracy, whereas in France, where formal instruction in reading is state-mandated at age five, thirty percent of the children experience reading problems.

If you're feeling pressured, and thereby pressuring your child to meet some artificial standard of academic success before he reaches the age of five or six, then you're definitely overdoing it. A recent Gallup survey of people who have attained eminence makes it very clear that parents of gifted children do not impose their own learning priorities on their children. They follow the child's lead. They read aloud, emphasize play, and provide a rich, stimulating environment. They are always available but never smothering and hovering. Formal instruction can wait!

WHERE CAN I GO FOR HELP?

"Okay," you respond, "so I'm totally responsible for my children's intellectual development and their subsequent success or failure in school. I'm supposed to provide them with a simulating learning environment. But if I overdo it, I might ruin them for life. How do I know just where to draw the line? What *are* the best things to do?"

I hope you'll find practical answers to these questions in Chapters 5 through 8.

What Every Parent Ought to Do

CHAPTER FIVE

Creating a Learning Environment in Your Home

CREATING A LEARNING ENVIRONMENT sounds suspiciously like hard work. Perhaps you envision setting up a home nursery school, as suggested in one book I read. The author recommended giving your "home preschool" a name and spending one hour per day with your children in programmed activities!

Or maybe you imagine purchasing hundreds of dollars of educational games and toys to enhance your children's intellectual development. Although many eager toy companies stand by, ready to take your money, that is not the primary emphasis of the home learning environment I am recommending.

The McEwan Home Learning Environment is child-centered. It has at its heart a family where learning is important, but not in a high-pressured or "educational" way. I hope that what you've read so far has given you a glimpse of what your family could become. More critical than just success in school is the sense of self-confidence and enthusiasm about learning that your children will develop, qualities that will spill over into all the dimensions of their lives. This plan I want to share has worked in my home, and I know it will work in yours.

There are five important basics to consider as you establish your learning environment:

- Parent behaviors—the most important ways to interact with your children for creating a learning environment.
- Needs of children—the critical needs that all children have relative to learning.
- Learning materials—the toys, books, arts and crafts supplies, and parent resources that are essential in your home.
- Learning skill areas—the key skill areas that all children need to develop for success in school.
- Learning activities—the activity areas in which your children need experiences to emerge as well-rounded students.

Once you understand the organizational structure of the home learning environment, you'll be able to plug into Chapters 6, 7, and 8, where you'll find specific activities for children on three age levels: babies, toddlers, and pre-schoolers.

BASIC PARENT BEHAVIORS FOR OPTIMUM LEARNING

I have already emphasized the critical role that the availability of parents plays in establishing a home learning environment. Availability means stopping to help children with a problem whenever they need help, but never hovering or encouraging them to concentrate all of their energies on you. It means responding as promptly and as often as possible to your children; making an effort to understand what they are doing and saying, and allowing them to make as many decisions about play as possible. I cannot emphasize strongly enough the importance of integrating these behaviors into your family life. Perhaps they come naturally to you, but if not, you need to consciously modify the way you behave.

The best way to understand these behaviors is to observe them in an actual family setting. Let's eavesdrop on a mother and child. Susan and Jason, her toddler, are in the living room. Susan is busy dusting, and Jason is looking out the picture window. He notices someone walking by and says one word, "Boy."

Susan responds, "I see the boy. That's John. He's on his way home from school. My goodness, look at what he's carrying. What do you think he has?"

She waits for a response, and when none is forthcoming she continues. "Those are books. My, but he looks tired. He's been working hard at school. Maybe he'll have some milk and cookies when he gets home."

The toddler picks up on only one idea in her statement. "I want a cookie," he declares.

Susan realizes that she has taken this conversation down the wrong path and responds, "Not right now, honey. We're going to eat dinner in just a little while. Let Mommy finish her dusting."

Susan has just demonstrated two essential parenting practices: *responding verbally to her child* and *trying to converse with her child*. Intent on her own work and thoughts, she could have chosen to ignore her child's one-word comment. Instead she utilized it as a potential learning experience. Let's continue our eavesdropping.

"We've had a good time this afternoon. Pick up your blocks now and get ready for dinner." When Jason complies, Susan continues, "Good job. You're a super helper today. It's fun to play with you."

In just a few words, she has *verbalized expectations, verbalized her approval*, and *verbalized affection to her child*— all critical behaviors in creating an optimum learning environment.

Jason tires of picking up his blocks and starts to wander away. Susan coaxes, "Come on, let's finish. If you don't get your blocks put away, we can't get dinner ready. Jason, are you listening to Mommy? If we don't put them away, they'll get lost." She stands and watches Jason while he put the blocks in the container.

In four short sentences, she has managed to include several more critical behaviors: *discouraging overdependence, encouraging the child's understanding of the reasons for her instructions, gaining the child's attention, persistence in*

61

enforcing directives, firmness, and *verbalizing the reasons for the child's obedience.*

The scene moves to the kitchen. Jason wants to help Mom fix dinner and impatiently pulls a chair toward the counter. Susan pats his head in approval and asks, "Why don't you put the napkins on the table?" *Expressing warmth, encouraging a child's independence, and training the child for self-direction* are three more important positive parenting behaviors.

We could eavesdrop for several more minutes and see other examples: *satisfying the child's needs, positive reinforcement, refraining from scolding,* and *respect for the child's reactions to a directive,* but I think you have the idea. The subtle exchanges between parent and child that take place dozens of times each day are the raw materials of the optimum learning environment.[1]

They seem so insignificant and mundane, these interludes of conversation and interaction. Yet these are the exchanges that enhance language development, convey expectations about behavior, satisfy children's needs, and consistently reinforce that they are important persons worthy of respect and attention. These are the exchanges that create an optimum learning environment.

When you are tempted to shortchange these interactions because of fatigue, frustration, impatience, or even because you underestimate your children's ability to understand or respond, remember, these are the glue of your learning environment. Research says so, and knowledgeable mothers everywhere will confirm it.

BASIC NEEDS OF CHILDREN

The needs of your children should also be considered when creating your home learning environment. Children want to play, they want to be on the go, they want to do things for themselves, they want to explore and find out, they want to make and grow things, they want to hear songs and stories.

Young children approach life on a sensory and motor level. They learn through touching, seeing, hearing, manipulating, and moving. They need activities that are spontaneous, things to do that meet the needs of the moment—and they need a wide variety of them.

Your goal as a parent is to get your child to do the work of play. Parents should simply provide the materials, the support, encouragement, assistance, and the consultation. Beware of activities that have you doing it all! The focus of the learning environment should be on learning through play, not on learning through direct teaching.

Through play children learn a variety of things:
- to control their bodies and develop physical strength
- to express their feelings
- to develop sensory awareness
- to practice problem solving
- to develop alternate ways of communicating
- to develop imagination and creativity
- to practice concentration and increase their attention span[2]
- to organize their environment
- to have fun and relax
- to form social relationships.[3]

BASIC LEARNING MATERIALS

In the chapters that follow, you will find out how to assemble a basic toy box, a library, a set of arts and crafts materials, and a parent reference library for each age level: babies, toddlers, and preschoolers. These recommendations will help you create a rich and stimulating environment, and provide everything you and your child will need to learn together.

Toys should be of high quality, safe, age-appropriate, and creative. Of course you'll have a few toys with batteries, flashing lights, or television themes, but try to maintain a good balance. You'll also need toys that stimulate symbolic play (let's pretend, construction, artwork); toys that stimulate intellectual development (games, shape sorters); toys that help children develop physical skills (scooters and tricycles); and my favorite category, toys for the sole purpose of loving and hugging (dolls and stuffed animals).

Each category has its place in your children's development, so be sure to develop a well-rounded collection. You'll be doing your children a real disservice if you focus only on "toys that teach" to the exclusion of toys that they can use to develop imagination and creativity.

All children need to have their own personal copies of *books* to read and reread. *How to Raise a Reader* suggests hundreds of books that are appropriate for reading aloud. Naturally you won't be able to purchase them all, so a few basic favorites will be recommended for each age level.

The third category of materials in the home learning environment is *arts and crafts supplies*. Most often these supplies are simply "junk" from around the house—egg cartons, buttons, old magazines, pipe cleaners, carpet samples, shoelaces, felt, feathers, spools—but sometimes you'll have to purchase paints, paper, crayons, and markers. We'll suggest an appropriate "junk box" for each age level.

The final category of materials is *parent resource books*, an important source of help and suggestions. You can, of course, borrow these books from your library, but you may wish to purchase your favorites to consult at a moment's notice.

BASIC SKILLS AREAS

There are five basic skills areas in which children need to learn for school success: motor skills, perceptual skills, language skills, conceptual skills, and cognitive skills. These were explained in Chapter 3, so check back if you've forgotten.

Most of what your children are learning will fall into several of these skill areas. For example, if you are reading an alphabet book about animals that includes acting out animal movements and making animal sounds, your children will be learning in *all* of the basic skill areas. The important thing is that they are learning, not that you can describe and explain in which category the learning is taking place.

BASIC LEARNING ACTIVITIES

The final step in creating your home learning environment will be to enlarge your repertoire of suitable learning activities. Perhaps you're good at thinking on your feet. Perhaps you're a natural teacher and have more than enough ideas to capture those teachable moments. If so, then you probably can skip this section. But I must confess that I was always grateful when someone came up with a tried and true idea that I could borrow.

The categories are somewhat arbitrary and artificial, but the activities are guaranteed to work with a minimum of fuss and bother. You won't need to prepare lesson plans or worksheets ahead of time. You won't need to laminate skill cards or read tons of reference books. You will be able to do all of these quickly and easily, which is the way life needs to be if you're the parent of a child under five years of age.

The categories are these: language and concept development, reading and reading readiness, values, physical development and play activities, music, cooking and household fun, arts, crafts, and creativity, math and science, and field trips. You will find yourself personally attracted to one or more of the categories, based on your own talents and interests. But sample them all with your children to see where their talents and interests might lie.

Language Development—Children learn by listening to their adult role models. Although we never "teach" children to talk in the way we teach other skills like reading or writing, there is a considerable difference in the way different children grow up learning to talk. Some have excellent sentence structure, outstanding vocabularies, and faultless grammar; others do not.

Thought and language are closely related; children who can master the intricacies of the English language will be able to influence and control their environment in ways that the language deprived child can never consider. Good language development activities should always have the following characteristics:

- Encourage the rich, colorful, and precise use of words through modeling and practice.
- Neither push nor patronize the child.

- Encourage many forms of expression through the use of body language, facial expression, and noise as well as words.
- Offer children a varied and legitimate audience for their attempts to communicate.
- Listen to your children and respect their attempts to communicate as important and worthy.
- Recognize that it is harder to generate language than to receive it.[4]
- Keep your conversations natural and real.
- Ask lots of questions.
- Respect your children's wishes if they decide they don't want to talk at the moment.
- Probe more deeply by following up with your own opinions and questions.
- Repeat, recast, and expand your child's statements.[5]

Reading Aloud and Reading Readiness—The most important activity that any parent can do to stimulate a love for reading and to develop reading readiness skills is to read aloud. Although you'll want to choose books that represent the finest in children's literature, what you read is not nearly as important as the fact that you do read.

At our house, reading aloud was an integral part of every day. There were nights that I could scarcely keep my eyes open through one more reading of *Green Eggs and Ham*, but as I look at my teenagers today, eagerly checking books out of the library to find out about things they don't know, I'm grateful that I persevered.

In addition to reading aloud, there are dozens of other simple things that you and your children can do together to prepare them for the wonderful world of reading. Suggestions for reading activities will be provided for each age level in Chapters 6, 7, and 8.

Values—You can't help sharing your values with your children. Even if you don't consciously work at teaching a specific set of values, or mistakenly feel you want your children to make up their own minds about what to believe, what you do provides a ready role model, for better or worse. So why not decide as parents which values are most important in your family life and then consciously seek to build those values into all of your family learning activities?

A family therapist, Virginia Satir, has called what parents teach children about themselves, others, the world, and God, "the essential learnings."[6] Activities that promote the development of Christian values should be as much a part of your learning environment as reading, math, and science. If you want your children to be patient and gentle with younger siblings, if you want your children to be brave in the face of danger, if you want your children to be thoughtful of their parents, then you must teach these values on a regular basis.

Suggestions for teaching values at each age level will be given in Chapters 6, 7, and 8.

Physical Development and Outdoor Play—Although we never built a jungle gym or purchased a swing set for our backyard, my children were no strangers to exercising their muscles. Our town has an extensive network of parks and playgrounds, and we were almost daily visitors to one or another of them when weather permitted.

Since we were within walking distance of Kelly Park, we often took a lunch and combined our playtime with a picnic. I usually took along some sewing or a good book and was "available for help" when needed. I wanted my children to be responsible for their own decisions about how to play.

Unless the weather was sub-zero, we went outside for some type of activity every day. Bundling up two toddlers for a romp in the snow is only slightly less work than preparing for the Normandy invasion, but I felt that all of us, children and mom, needed to get out and breathe the fresh air. During warmer weather, the children explored the backyard, painted water pictures on the cement driveway, blew bubbles, watched the ants, raked leaves, rode Big Wheels, and bounced balls.

Music—The opportunity to make and listen to music should be part of all children's growing up experiences. Even if you're not musical yourself, that is no reason to deprive your children of a rich musical upbringing.

All children should have a drum, a xylophone, a music box, and an inexpensive record player. Tapping out rhythmic patterns on an oatmeal box drum; discovering that glasses filled with different quantities of water can play a familiar tune, and singing along with a favorite group are activities that even a musical illiterate can manage.

Cooking—A young mother I know jokingly says there are two ways to cook, "the fast way or with help." The kind of help she is talking about is help from her two young children. Of course, if you're in a hurry, cooking with kids can be a pain. But cooking together can also make beautiful memories.

My kids and I still talk about the gingerbread house we created together. This once-in-a-lifetime experience is preserved on film, but the best pictures are those in our mind's eye as we remember the spicy smell of gingerbread baking, the frosting smeared everywhere on the kitchen counter, and the candies we carefully chose to trim our masterpiece.

If you have to cook anyhow, and most of us still do, include your children in the process frequently. Children feel very competent and grown-up when they can help us in the kitchen. They learn reading, math, and self-help skills, all while making good things to eat . . . and an occasional mess.

Arts, Crafts, and Creativity—The creative genius of a child is not to be underestimated. Who but a child could take cardboard and masking tape and create a fleet of sailing ships that could join the British navy? Who but a child could take a gross of popsicle sticks and build skyscrapers to rival the Chicago skyline? Who but a child can turn feathers, sequins, and beans into a Thanksgiving turkey that looks good enough to eat?

As long as I supplied them with enough junk, my children were always ready to create something new. Perhaps it was because I never supplied them with the ideas, only the materials, that they seemed so creative. (Or perhaps it was because my own attempts at art were so feeble that my children felt free to shine!) Whatever the reason, I knew I could always count on at least sixty minutes of free time if I brought out the art box.

In addition to the traditional media like crayons, markers, paints, and clay, there are the dozens of materials around the house that inspire creativity. While the mess and confusion that accompany such projects may tempt you to concentrate on something less damaging to your new kitchen carpet, think about all that your children are learning when they experiment with art: manual dexterity, observing and understanding why and how things happen, eye-hand coordination, sense of balance, using tools, memory, concentration, perseverance, measuring, drawing, classifying, understanding colors, shapes, sizes, and relationships, identifying objects and developing vocabulary, sensitivity to art and beauty, self-confidence, and problem solving.[7]

A variety of activities to develop just these skills will be suggested for each age level in the chapters that follow.

Math and Science—Mathematics and science have a foreboding sound to them. But even if you didn't get past algebra in high school, there is no reason that you cannot raise a child with an interest and bent for mathematics and science. The experiences are everywhere—in the kitchen, the backyard, and even in the bathtub. Once you're aware of the possibilities, you'll be surprised at the fun you can have while learning.

Sorting, comparing, measuring, and counting—all are mathematical activities that you do on a daily basis. Before you peel the potatoes, sort them into piles of small, medium, and large. Count them. Find the biggest and the smallest potato. Find the potato that has the roundest shape and the one that is oblong. You can probably think of several more games to play with your dinner, but the potatoes will never get peeled if you get carried away.

Growing herbs from seeds, watching an ant hill, observing birds and squirrels in the backyard, all are exciting science activities. Choose books to read aloud that answer the questions from nature that you can't answer. Check in the encyclopedia to find out where the sun goes at night and why birds can fly. You'll learn right along with your children.

Math concepts that should be explored with your child include: relationships (How does one item relate to another? Which is big, bigger, biggest?), categorizing, measurement, and patterns.[8]

Field Trips—Traditional field trips take place in a school setting. You no doubt remember getting on a big yellow bus and spending a day at the zoo or a local museum. Field trips for young children are similar, but you don't have to travel to exotic locations to have your excursion qualify.

My friend Dotty and I planned a field trip to Marshall Field's, that venerable Chicago institution, almost once a week when weather permitted and all of our children were healthy. We packed our four children (all under three) into one car, along with assorted strollers and diaper bags, and set out for Oakbrook, an elegant shopping center about fifteen minutes away. Each day from 10:00-11:30, coffee was served in the Oak Room.

The first time we made the trip, I'm sure the waitresses trembled in their sensible oxfords to see our entourage of babies and toddlers, but we were undaunted. We settled everyone in high chairs and booster seats and proceeded to order pecan coffee cake and chocolate milk all around. Those in the group who were old enough to walk made their way to the elegantly appointed serving table to choose their own piece of coffee cake from the buffet. They balanced their plates in tiny hands and nervously carried their treats back to the table. Those still in high chairs were served by the waitress. After we became regulars and they got to know us, the waitresses always brought special treats for the children.

Other field trips included the zoo, local parks, the library, the swimming pool, McDonald's for hamburgers, or Big Boy for their famous grilled cheese sandwiches. We used these field trips as learning experiences. We met other people, we saw new sights, and we kept our daily routine lively and interesting. We visited Cantigny, a local attraction featuring a museum, formal gardens, and a wonderful collection of indestructible tanks and machinery for the children to climb and play upon.

Your own community has its own set of interesting locations to captivate your children. Other suggestions appropriate to the various age levels will be made in the chapters that follow.

You should now be ready to create your own home learning environment. Let's review the recipe one last time:

Mix a generous amount of parental attention and availability with equal parts of books, toys, and arts and crafts supplies. Add a pinch of creativity, all the patience you have on hand, an ample amount of discipline, and allow to age in the warmth and security of a loving home.

Sprinkle every day with reading aloud, heart-to-heart conversations, a little cooking, an activity or two for learning fun, a trip around the neighborhood to see what's happening, and a generous portion of good old fashioned play.

Your children will be ready for school success at about the age of five, but test for doneness and don't hesitate to leave at home for another year of warmth and security if needed.

1. Levenstein, Phyllis. *Messages from Home*, Columbus, Ohio, Ohio State University Press, 1988, pp. 56-59.
2. Saunders, Jacqulyn with Pamela Espeland. *Bringing Out the Best*, Minneapolis, Minnesota, Free Spirit Publishing Company, 1986, p. 129.
3. Rubin, Richard R., Fisher, John J., Doering, Susan G., *Your Toddler*, New York, Macmillan,1980, p. 185.
4. Saunders, op. cit., pp. 70-71.
5. Rubin, Richard R., and John J. Fisher, *Your Preschooler*, New York, Macmillan, 1982, pp. 58-59.
6. Satir, Virginia, *Peoplemaking*, Palo Alto, California, Science and Behavior Books, 1972.
7. Taetzsch, Sandra Zeitlin, and Taetzsch, Lyn, *Pre-School Games and Activities*, Belmont, California, Pitman Learning, Inc., 1974, p. 64.
8. Saunders, op. cit., pp. 99-100.

CHAPTER SIX

Babies: Kids Who Are Crawling

IN AN ANNOYINGLY NONCHALANT TONE OF VOICE, my pediatrician assured me that Patrick would—probably—outgrow his relentless crying around dinner time before he was three months old. He advised me to "ignore it."

If I had actually been at his office, perhaps I would have pressed the issue, but I was one of dozens of callers to the physician's hot line that morning and I could hear the impatience in his voice; he was eager to move on to the next caller. No doubt the good doctor had never listened to a baby with colic for more than five or ten minutes.

I hung up in frustration and despair. Three months of coping with a screaming baby and a fussy two year old while trying to cook dinner stretched endlessly before me. Surely there must be something I could do to soothe this troubled child.

I began to experiment with different locations, different sounds, and different positions. Beethoven or the Beatles? The crib or the cradle? Upstairs or down? A dark room or bright lights? I eventually found the answer. Patrick was stretched out on his baby blanket in the living room, where the late afternoon sun cast interesting shadows on the wall. The celery-colored carpet was soft and inviting. Soothing classical music played on the radio. I placed a stuffed animal nearby. Suddenly Patrick seemed to relax. His tense little body unstiffened. Perhaps it was my imagination, but he seemed to be watching the shadows and listening to the music. He was distracted from his physical misery by the environment.

Perhaps it is only coincidental that Patrick still gravitates to this same location each day to do his homework and relax after a busy day at school. Instead of rattles and baby bottles, high school texts and a well worn gym bag now cover the floor. But there is something about this corner of the room that enables him to be organized and attentive. In the very location that he watched the shadows as an infant, he studies for final exams as a teenager. Even though he has a desk and study lamp in his bedroom, his best work is done here, surrounded by old friends.

Creating a learning environment for your baby in the first year begins with finding stimulating and comforting places for her to be before she can move around on her own, and quickly moves to the challenge of child-proofing your house from the eager and inquisitive crawler and walker.

From birth to three months, your baby will learn to hold her head up and begin to bat at objects with her hands. Between three and six months of age she will learn to reach for objects, grasp and let go of favorite toys, and roll over and sit with support. By six months of age, she will sit alone, begin to creep, and use her thumb and forefinger to pick up small objects. By the time you're lighting the candles on the birthday cake for her one year party, your baby will most likely be a whirlwind of activity, creeping, pulling herself to a standing position and poking and prodding everything in sight. Many babies are already walking at this age, although just as many continue to crawl for several months.

In this chapter you will find ideas for assembling a basic toy box, library, set of arts and crafts materials, and parent reference library to help you create an optimum learning environment for your baby's first year. There are dozens of suggestions for activities. You won't be able to do them all, nor should you necessarily. They aren't designed to be done in any particular order. They aren't meant to be done on a day by day basis. Some will become a daily part of your routine until you and your baby tire of them. Others you may find to be too difficult or easy for you and your baby. Experiment, adapt, and enjoy!

THE TOY BOX

If you consult a book devoted solely to selecting toys for your child, you may come away feeling slightly depressed about the task that lies ahead. The authors will suggest hundreds of possibilities. A visit to your local toy store will do little to alleviate your confusion, particularly if you visit a large discount store that sells nothing but toys. There are dozens of aisles, and the shelves reach to the ceiling. Add to that the pressure you feel to choose just the right "educational" toys, and your task seems impossible.

But don't be discouraged! Many of the toys your child will use doing this first year will come as baby gifts, and others will be found right in your own home. In any case, remember that during your child's first year, *you* are your baby's best toy. Grab hold of those tiny fingers and say a nursery rhyme. Make a game out of touching baby's face. Lose your inhibitions and have fun!

TOYS YOU CAN BUY

Mobiles. Choose one that expresses your personality! Make sure it is large enough and bright enough that your baby can see it. Mount it on the crib or playpen and then talk about it with your baby. If you really want to go first-class, purchase one with a music box or one that is activated by your child's touching or pulling. Some parents suspend a stainless steel mirror above baby's crib or attach it to the crib rail or changing table so she can see herself in it. Move the mobile or mirror to different locations around the bed for variety.

Rattles. Although simple and old-fashioned, the rattle is still a staple of every first year toy box. I always tie one to the ribbon of gifts I give to newborns.

Cradle gym. Child development specialists are divided on their recommendations regarding cradle gyms. Little hands and feet can easily become caught in the rings and apparatus that come attached to this toy, so shop carefully and provide close supervision.

Stuffed toys. If you've visited a department store lately, you know that stuffed animals are big business. I've always accused my husband of suffering stuffed animal deprivation as a child, since he seemed to lose all sense of judgment when he approached Marshall Field's stuffed animal section. You don't have to spend a fortune or get more than one or two. The teddy bear you choose today may well be around for decades.

Rubber squeeze toys. These toys (balls, blocks, animals, and dolls) will give you lots of ideas for playing with your baby. They come in every shape, color, and size, but the basic noise is the same—an annoying squeak that babies seem to love.

Teethers. Babies have an insatiable need to put things in their mouths and chew. Provide them with lots of colorful teething implements. I used to tie one of my daughter's favorites around my neck during the Sunday morning service. It made a charming necklace for me, and whenever she dropped it, I didn't have to retrieve it from the dirty floor.

Push-over toys. These toys pop back to a standing position when shoved. They are a perfect way to teach that every action has a reaction. They usually come with music or noise of some sort, adding a further attraction.

Shape-sorting toys. As your baby gets close to a year old, a shape sorting box will begin to intrigue her. Don't expect your baby to immediately master the concept. This will be a challenging toy for many months to come.

Nesting and stacking toys. Major toy manufacturers provide several variations on these two themes. They come in colorful shapes and sizes and will provide hours of fun.

Bath toys. Make a wonderful experience even more enjoyable by providing some floating toys.

TOYS YOU ALREADY OWN

Pictures, *posters*, and *wallpaper*. Some new parents hang wallpaper with Disney characters or nursery rhyme motifs. Being a little lazy, Dick and I decided we didn't want to paper more than once in ten years, so for Patrick's room we hung paper with many different kinds of sailing ships. The paper is still hanging and is quite suitable for a young man of eighteen. What we did change quite often were the pictures and posters hanging in his room. We also borrowed mini-art prints from our public library and put them in a wooden display rack on the table or dresser.

Old magazines and newspapers. When your baby begins to sit up by herself, give her old magazines and newspapers to tear, crumble, and feel. The sensory experiences are well worth the mess. Just remember to closely supervise this play experience to keep eager babies from sampling the culinary delights of newsprint.

Kitchen utensils. Pots, pans, wooden ladles, and other kitchen implements are wonderful to bang, stack, feel, hold, and lift. Rather than making the kitchen cabinets off limits to your inquisitive crawler, create a drawer just for her. You can duplicate many of the more expensive toys simply by using your plastic storage containers, nesting mixing bowls, and measuring spoons.

Busy box. You can buy busy boxes that provide many activities for eager hands, but you can also create one. Simply fill a container (a large plastic mixing bowl will do just fine) with all kinds of interesting things: an empty tape spool, a small plastic soap dish, a spoon, a lid, a metal mirror, etc.). This is a perfect way to utilize all that "junk" you've been collecting. Just remember that whatever you include will find its way into your baby's mouth.

Radio, record player, cassette player. Expose your children to music, both adult and children's. Play records of various types and see if they have a preference for one type of music over another. Check out records and cassettes from your public library. Tape record some soothing sounds or purchase cassettes with ocean noises. Someone I know taped the sound of her washing machine, claiming that the churning, sloshing sound had a comforting effect on her infant.

Wind chime. A wind chime near an open window can be an intriguing sound for an infant.

YOUR BABY'S LIBRARY

Books that children will enjoy during the first year don't have developed plots or stories. They contain few if any words and have bright, realistic pictures. A child's first books are usually made of cloth or heavy board so that tiny hands (and mouths) can handle them. They contain familiar objects and animals that children will recognize. Books with pop ups and special surprises are especially fun if read with supervision. In the following list, Christian books are indicated with an asterisk.

I GO TO CHURCH* (Marian Bennett, Illustrated by Mary Ann Dorr, Standard, 1985)—One of the "My Shape Book" series, this board book is shaped like a church steeple. The text and illustrations are appropriate for the very young child. Other titles in the series includes *Shapes and Things, My Family and Friends, Animals in the Ark, Bible Story Favorites,* and *God's Rainbow of Colors.*

THE BABY JESUS* (Carolyn Bracken, Thomas Nelson, 1985)—Part of the Tuck-a-Toy series, this cloth book has been designed to develop manual dexterity as your baby learns about some "special babies." Others in the series are *The Baby Moses, The Baby Bear,* and *The Special Baby.* In each book, the featured baby is attached with a colorful ribbon and can be tucked into a special place provided on the front cover. Young ones delight in putting Baby Jesus or Baby Moses in and out of their special book.

GOD MADE ALL THE COLORS* (Linden Evans, Lion, 1979)—Buy this series as part of your baby's first exposure to books. (*God Made Them All, Who Made Friends? Who Made Mothers and Fathers? Great and Small,* and *Bright and Beautiful.*) The illustrations are whimsical, the colors are brilliant, and the text is simple, but meaningful.

POEMS TO READ TO THE VERY YOUNG (Josette Frank, Illustrated by Eloise Wilkins, Random House, 1982)— This should be the first poetry collection you buy. Expressive illustrations by Eloise Wilkins bring to life the poetry of such favorites as A. A. Milne, Christina Rosetti, and Robert Louis Stevenson. There are many poems by more contemporary poets as well.

A CHILD'S BOOK OF PRAYERS* (Michael Hague, Holt, Rinehart and Winston, 1985)—The traditional childhood prayers are reverently illustrated with five colors, gold borders, and easy-to-read type.

MOTHER GOOSE* (Michael Hague, Holt, Rinehart and Winston, 1984)—This collection of classic nursery rhymes is beautifully illustrated in a soft, old-fashioned style. Since there is only one rhyme and illustration per page, the volume is especially appropriate for the younger child. An index of first lines is very helpful. If you don't know many nursery rhymes, this is a good place to begin.

MY BIBLE BOOK OF RHYMES* (John Knapp II, Illustrated by Dianne Turner Deckert, David C. Cook, 1987)— This unique collection of Bible stories in verse is arranged chronologically from Genesis to Revelation. Knapp is a master poet and his verses will become favorites in Christian families. The illustrations are joyful and make the biblical characters seem real to children.

PAT THE BUNNY (Dorothy Kunhardt, Golden, 1962)— This classic is a popular gift because it appeals to the child's senses. Patting the furry bunny, smelling the scented flower, and playing peek-a-boo with the child in the book involve your child in many ways.

READ ALOUD BIBLE STORIES, Volumes 1 and 2* (Ella K. Lindvall, Illustrated by H. Kent Puckett [Volume 1] and Ken Renczenski [Volume 2], Moody Press, 1982 and 1985)—The stories have been written for the interest level and attention span of the very young child. The illustrations do an excellent job of telling the stories graphically. Your child may not do more than look at the pictures and listen to a simple retelling, but you'll use this book for many years.

WHO (Leo Lionni, Pantheon, 1983)—This wordless board book is part of a series. Other titles are, of course, *What*, *Where*, and *When*. The characteristic Lionni mice drawings are found on each page with a person, object, location, or event. The child and parent can together discover who, what, where, or when.

ARTS AND CRAFTS SUPPLIES

Perhaps you're wondering what kinds of arts and crafts supplies to collect when your child is still so young. Although these materials won't be used for activities that you might traditionally think of as art, it's not too early to begin letting your child know that fun can be found in all sorts of materials—not just expensive ones from the toy store. Free play with the following materials is a precursor to creating more complicated works of art with more sophisticated media.

Collect all kinds of discarded *spools*. I contacted my local tailor when I couldn't collect enough from my own sewing activities. They make wonderful stacking toys and can also be threaded on heavy cord to make necklaces, trains, and whatever else your imagination dictates.

Small *aluminum tins* that used to contain frozen tarts or chicken pot pies are another source of fun. They can be threaded, twisted, worn as hats, or taped together with noisemakers inside. Be creative!

Yogurt containers with lids make wonderful building blocks. If you use different brands or eat many different flavors, you can also begin to teach sorting as you stack all of the blueberry or cherry flavors in one place.

Collect *fabric samples* of different colors and textures. They are fun to feel and can later be used to make collages.

There's nothing like dozens of *boxes of different sizes and shapes* to bring out the creative genius in a child. Just stacking and knocking them down can entertain a child for at least as long as it takes to use the bathroom uninterrupted.

PARENT RESOURCE BOOKS

Parenting is a challenging task. That's why I'm including some resource books to help you through the early years. You will find that most of them will continue to be helpful even after your children are well past their first birthdays. You can borrow these books from your public library, but you may want to purchase your favorites for easy reference.

INFANTS AND MOTHER: DIFFERENCES IN DEVELOPMENT (T. Berry Brazelton, Delacorte Press, 1983)—I must have taken the first edition of this book out of the library a dozen times in 1970, for it was the most comforting book I had ever read. Dr. Brazelton's warm, supportive style has been a favorite for moms since it appeared. This new edition makes allowances for the changes in contemporary lifestyles by also focusing on fathers and working couples.

SMART TOYS: FOR BABIES FROM BIRTH TO TWO (Kent Garland Burtt, Illustrated by Tricia Taggart, Harper & Row, 1984)—If you're looking for a more extensive review of various toys, this is a good place to find the information.

THE POWER OF PLAY (Frank and Theresa Caplan, Anchor Press, 1973)—Play is the work of the very young child. The Caplans discuss how play contributes not only to early learning, but also to social and emotional development.

*THE COMPLETE BOOK OF BABY AND CHILD CARE FOR CHRISTIAN PARENTS** (Grace H. and Herbert L. Ketterman, Fleming H. Revell Co., 1982)— Answers the most common questions about child development from a Christian perspective.

HOW TO RAISE A READER* (Elaine K. McEwan, David C. Cook, 1987)—Contains age-graded read-aloud suggestions for children from birth to age twelve.

A PARENT'S GUIDE TO THE FIRST THREE YEARS (Burton L. White, Prentice-Hall, Inc., 1980)—Read this book early and often. White's research is important and practical!

LEARNING ACTIVITIES

In this chapter and the two that follow, we will discuss each of the learning activities introduced in Chapter 5 as they apply to the different stages of your child's development. Each activity will become a section unto itself, containing a number of alternatives for you to consider and try with your children. The first one, as you may remember, was language development.

LANGUAGE AND CONCEPT DEVELOPMENT

Since the beginning of time, parents have engaged in language and concept development activities without even knowing what they were doing. Because babies are so much fun, most parents lose their inhibitions at once and start making strange noises and funny faces to entertain their offspring. They talk to their babies, play those time honored games of pat-a-cake and peek-a-book, and carry them from room to room.

"Language and concept development activities" are really nothing more than good old-fashioned fun with your baby. But if babies have typically made you nervous, and you're feeling a bit uptight about just how to go about it, here are some suggestions.

Imitations. Try to get your baby to imitate what you do. Use different facial expressions like broad smiles, a surprised look, a hearty laugh, a furrowed brow, or a wrinkled nose. For variation, use nonsense syllables or sounds. When your young one is a little older, try simple hand movements like pointing, waving good-bye, patting, clapping, making a fist and opening it, or touching your finger to your nose. Head movements like nodding or shaking your head "no" are also fun to try. Naturally you won't do all of these at the same time, nor become discouraged when your budding genius doesn't respond right away. Do these naturally as part of your daily routine.

Talking. In addition to talking to your baby whenever she is awake and alert, give names and labels to things around you. Carry your child from room to room as you move about the house. If she is awake, keep her isolation in a crib or playpen to the barest minimum. Recite simple poems, nursery rhymes, and nursery games. (See the section below for more details.) Name body parts as you touch them or count fingers and toes.

Peek-a-boo. This game has been played for generations and continues to delight young children. Variations include the "where games" like "Where is Daddy?" and "Where's the doggie?" Play the game in the bathtub by dropping a washcloth over a floating toy and asking your child where it went.

Nursery rhymes and games. If you didn't grow up learning the following favorite rhymes and games, then by all means begin teaching them to your child today. The rhyme and repetition are wonderful for language development, but the best part about them is the fun you'll have. We don't have room to print all of them, but here some favorites from the McEwan family:

At bath time be sure to sing the following (to the tune of "Here We Go 'Round the Mulberry Bush"):

> *This is the way we wash our face,*
> *Wash our face, wash our face.*
> *This is the way we wash our face,*
> *So early in the morning.*

And as you count those pudgy little toes, how about reciting this favorite? Be sure to start with the big toe.

> *This little piggy went to market.*
> *This little piggy stayed home.*
> *This little piggy had roast beef.*

This little piggy had none.
And this little piggy cried "Wee-wee-wee"
All the way home.

When you're bouncing your baby on your knee, accompany the ride with this familiar rhyme:

Ride a cock horse to Banbury Cross
To see a fine lady upon a white horse.
With rings on her fingers and bells on her toes
She shall make music wherever she goes.

There are some who eschew the following rhyme, finding it scary and violent, but my babies enjoyed playing it over and over, and I find their psyches remarkably unscarred. Of course when the cradle does fall, you're always there to catch the baby.

Rock-a-bye baby, on the tree top,
When the wind blows, the cradle will rock.
When the bough breaks, the cradle will fall,
And down will come baby, cradle and all.

When your child learns to pat-a-cake, you'll feel as though she's ready for kindergarten. You'll want her to show off her new found talent for everyone, and she usually will . . . when no one is looking. Of course you'll do the motions while you recite the words.

Pat-a-cake; pat-a-cake,
Baker's man.
Bake me a cake, as fast as you can.
Prick it and pat it, and mark it with a B
And put it in the oven for Baby and me.

Another silly game to play goes like this:

There was a little mouse
And he had a little house.
And he lived—up—here!

At "here" your hand travels up your baby's arm and tickles her under the arm or chin. Always be careful when tickling infants or young children that you are sensitive to a real dislike of this kind of play. Make your tickling gentle and fun.

READING AND READING READINESS

Reading aloud. Begin reading aloud right away. Of course you probably won't hold a picture book in front of your tiny infant, but when you're rocking late at night, retell some of your favorite stories. Sing hymns or songs. Recite poetry or nursery rhymes. Hearing the English language with all of its beauty and rhythm will set the stage for reading in later years.

Picture talk. As soon as your baby is old enough to notice pictures, begin using picture talk. Identify, locate, and talk about the people and objects in the pictures. Ask questions such as "Who is this?" "What is this?" and "Where is the doggy?" and then answer those questions. Soon your child will be answering you.

As your child gains experience, your discussion of pictures can move away from simple identification to more complex activities like finding, recalling, and evaluating actions in the pictures. At first your child will probably grow restless and bored after several minutes of picture talk, but many children have long attention spans when the subjects are interesting.

Don't use baby talk and don't be afraid to do some comparing, classifying, or explaining. A parent can never be sure just how much a child is absorbing, so do what comes naturally. Do this on a daily basis!

Auditory awareness. A crucial part of reading readiness is the ability to distinguish various sounds. Begin making your child aware of sounds in the environment by identifying those you hear and talking about them. Barking dogs, sirens, voices, appliances, telephones, and doorbells are all everyday sounds that can turn into learning experiences for your child.

VALUES

We usually don't think about imparting values to infants, but research shows that infancy is just the time that a child's value structure is being formed. The more you touch, handle, and play with your baby, the stronger her attachment to you will be. If you are gentle, sensitive, accepting, and caring, these values will be gradually imparted to your child. Infancy is not too early to begin treating your child with respect.

Manners. Begin almost immediately to model the politeness and respect for your child that you want her to have as an adult. Saying "please" and "thank you" in your interactions with your infant may seem unnecessary, but you'll never know at what point she will begin to learn that these phrases are a key part of positive relationships with others.

Prayers. Along with reading Bible stories, poems, and nursery rhymes, introduce simple prayers. Each night as you tuck your child into bed, take time to recite one of your favorites. Or use several different ones to vary your routine.

Responsiveness. Critical to the ability to interact with others and respond to their needs is the development of trust. As parents are responsive to their babies' needs, so will those children develop the ability to be caring adults. You need not worry that meeting your children's needs for cuddling and warmth during the first months of life will result in a "spoiled child." The more contact and interaction they have in the early months with warm and loving parents, the stronger the likelihood that they will develop kindness, sharing, sympathy, and consideration.

PHYSICAL DEVELOPMENT AND PLAY ACTIVITIES

There are many wonderful games and activities that stimulate physical and mental development while providing just plain fun. Your children may not respond with equal enthusiasm to all, so find your favorites.

What do you feel? I never systematically gathered all of these items at one time for an organized activity, but I did play this game whenever we encountered a new sensory experience. Here are just a few of the things you can use to play: baby blanket (smooth binding, soft wool or nylon), pieces of crinkly paper, burlap, velvet, silk, leather, wood, snow, ice cube, slightly warm hot water bottle, a flower petal, a dog or cat, Daddy's whiskers, grass, the cold tile floor, the warm carpet. Use every new object you encounter to play the game and talk about what you're feeling.

Reach for it. Keep your baby on a clean floor in a warm, safe room where she can practice pushing herself up or moving about. Position a soft ball or fabric blocks that make noise within reaching distance so she'll be intrigued enough to try to reach it.

Bathtub games. Water lends itself to loads of extra fun. Just have plenty of towels around to mop up the mess. Pretend your baby's washcloth is the fish. Swirl it around in the tub and encourage your baby to grab it. Cover a favorite bathtub toy with the washcloth and see if your baby can find it. Pour water from a cup and see if your baby can catch it in her hands. When she's even more coordinated, see if she can pour water from her cup into yours. Use the rhyme mentioned earlier to sing about each of the body parts as you wash them.

Changing table challenge. Changing diapers will be much more enjoyable if you play little games or otherwise occupy your active baby. Before or after the change, hold your baby's feet as you pedal her legs gently. Before long she'll be pressing her legs against your hands with great vigor. See if she can catch your forefinger before you take it away. Let her win at least half of the time!

Paper fun. Use newspaper, magazines, waxed paper, typing paper, shopping bags, deflated mylar balloons, or an old telephone book for noisy paper fun. This can be very exciting for a five or six month old, but be sure to supervise closely.

Outdoor fun. Visit the playground and sit in the sandbox. If your baby is crawling, make some knee pads for him. My son, Patrick, didn't walk until about fourteen months, so I fashioned some pads and sewed them into the knees of his overalls. He was off and crawling over concrete and anything else in sight.

Take your baby outside at every opportunity. For the young baby, park the carriage outside where he can see the leaves, sunshine, changing clouds in the sky, feel the warm breezes, and hear the birds singing.

Hang on tight. Gather together as many different long, narrow objects as you can. We used rattle handles, toothbrushes, Lincoln Logs, blocks, and unsharpened pencils.

Hold out the object in front of your baby and say, "What's this? Hang on tight." If she gets a good grip, play a little tug of war. Talk about what you are holding and whether it feels smooth or rough.

Hide and seek. Children are fascinated by objects, people, or sounds that appear and then disappear. You can play this game in dozens of different ways with different objects and children never seem to tire of it. Change hiding places or objects, and the game will be brand new. In the beginning, hide the object as your child watches and ask her to find it. Before long she'll have the idea.

Obstacle course. Once your baby begins to creep and crawl you can create an obstacle course around which she must navigate to retrieve a favorite toy. Use furniture cushions, boxes, or pillows. Don't make the first course too difficult, but once she has the idea, throw in a few challenges.

Stack and knock. This game is good for as long as you're willing to build towers. Build a block tower (soft blocks are probably best at this point) and show your baby how to knock it down. In the early stages, you'll do all the building and he'll do all the knocking.

Fill the bowl. Drop wooden blocks one at time into a metal mixing bowl or tin cannister. Help your baby drop them in. While you're dropping them, name the colors or count them. Although your child isn't formally learning colors or math, include the concepts as you talk together.

Catch me games. As soon as your child can move about with ease, play simple games of tag. You can either try to catch your child ("I'm going to get you") or she can try to catch you ("Catch me if you can"). Make sure you let her win at least half of the time.

Follow the wiggly line. Wiggle a piece of colored rope or string along the ground like a snake and entice your baby to follow you.

MUSIC

In the early months of your baby's life, play music for at least one to two hours per day. Use tapes, records, radio, music boxes, your own singing, and the piano or another musical instrument if you play. Play records of various types to see if your child has a preference for different types of music. If you want your child to grow up enjoying classical music, now is a good time to start playing it.

Encourage your child to clap or sing along to records, particularly if there are motions or dance steps that accompany the song. All of these activities will build not only an appreciation of music, but a sense of rhythm as well.

COOKING AND HOUSEHOLD FUN

Although your child from birth to one probably won't be helping out in the kitchen, make sure she knows she is welcome when you are working there. When you are mixing up a recipe, give her mixing bowls and spoons to play with on the floor. When you are using appliances like the blender or mixer, hold her in your arms so she can hear the sounds and see the action. Give her a special drawer or cabinet that has her own set of kitchen tools and she will leave you free to get your cooking done in peace.

ARTS, CRAFTS, AND CREATIVITY

Although you won't see signs of a budding Van Gogh or Andrew Wyeth in your baby's first year, there are some simple activities that are art related and fun.

Finger painting with food. Since children enjoy playing with food anyway, why not give them your assistance and permission? This edible finger paint is guaranteed to bring out creativity in the high chair set. Mix one egg yolk, two tablespoons water, and one or two drops of food coloring. Use a *very* washable surface and prepare for a bath soon after!

Edible play dough. If you want to try your hand at some simple modeling and are worried about your sculptor eating the clay, mix up a batch of this edible play dough: One 8 oz. jar of peanut butter, six tablespoons honey, and three cups of powdered milk.

Art appreciation. Now is the time to build appreciation for color and design. Hang art prints around your home. You need not buy original art or spend a great deal on frames; you can even borrow prints from many public libraries. Children who live with good art develop an innate sense of taste and appreciation that no college course in art appreciation can guarantee.

Your baby's first masterpiece. Children are ready for crayons at about ten months. For heaven's sake, don't use coloring books. The drawings look much too good and intimidate the average child.

Show her how to scribble, and then provide lots of cheap newsprint drawing paper and different colored crayons. Hang up her work on the refrigerator. Do make sure you keep the crayons under lock and key when she's not supervised, or you might have your own personal art gallery courtesy of your resident artist.

MATH AND SCIENCE
Math and science sound like pretty serious topics for babies, but as you begin to develop language and concepts, include the vocabulary of mathematics and science as well.

Who is taller? Play this game and learn the concepts of big and little, and tall and short.

Which is longer? Talk about trucks, trains, and buses, or carrots, celery, and cucumbers. There are dozens of comparisons you can make every day to teach this concept.

Which holds more? Play this game in the bathtub with different size containers.

Which is heavier? Find out by lifting various toys or objects.

Word pairs that suggest games. Consider the following word pairs and take opportunities to compare objects and experiences from everyday life to illustrate them: dark and light; hot and cold; loud and soft; hard and soft; sharp and dull; open and closed; straight and crooked; smooth and bumpy; and up and down. The best way to teach concepts to children is through constant exposure to concrete examples. Don't expect that your child will understand after you tell him once or twice. And above all, don't begin quizzing your preschooler for the "right" answer.

Counting. Many counting rhymes and games introduce the concept of numbers. "One two, buckle my shoe" is a favorite. Use the following vocabulary when comparing groups of objects: more, less, fewer, and the same.

Young children learn one to one correspondence by counting just two things. They need to understand two before they can move to three. They need to understand three before moving to four, and so on.

FIELD TRIPS

Don't be afraid to take your children places. Just make sure that they get nourishment and naps on time and you'll get along fine.

Restaurants. Trips to inexpensive restaurants give you a break from cooking, and with planning can be delightful learning experiences. Just be prepared for those unexpected emergencies like spilled food, broken dishes, and crying babies. Learn to hold your head high and be profuse with your apologies.

Zoos. For a baby in a stroller, a short trip to a petting farm or a zoo can be a time of wonder and excitement. Buy a balloon, tie it to the stroller, visit only the animals that are large enough and interesting enough to command his attention, and make your trip short enough so that all concerned will have a good time.

Art and crafts fairs. Shopping centers are filled with art fairs, and they make perfect outings for kids in strollers. Unusual sculptures and wild avant garde paintings are adored by children. And they will love the attention they get from all of the adults in attendance.

Grocery stores. Make an outing to the grocery store a field trip rather than a dreaded weekly occurrence. Make sure your baby has had enough to eat, or plan a treat as part of the trip. I often bought a box of animals crackers which lasted until our shopping was over. Whether your child is in an infant seat or firmly buckled in the shopping cart, talk about what you are buying and where you are going.

Play groups. Because I was a FEMALE (Formerly Employed Mother At Loose Ends) when my children were small, I needed adult contact on a daily basis. I sought out friends with young children, and we got together often so that we could enjoy each other's company. These outings provided opportunities to explore other houses, eat lunches at other tables, and play with other children and their toys.

Parks, playgrounds, swimming pools. We are fortunate to live in a community that provides many wonderful parks with equipment for very small children and a wading pool that is perfect for hot summer cooling off. Winter or summer, outdoor field trips should be part of almost every day.

Libraries. Even though your child is not yet choosing her own books, make a weekly trip to the library to browse through the children's section. Get acquainted with the vast array of children's literature and take several home each week for reading aloud. Introduce yourself and your child to the children's librarian. She'll soon be calling you by name and recommending good read-alouds. Don't forget the church library as a valuable source of Christian read-alouds.

Shopping centers. An enclosed mall gives you free entertainment for as long as you can last—store windows, fountains, concession stands, and interesting people. Just don't impose an adult shopping agenda on your baby, and you'll get along fine!

You won't be able to do everything listed here at once, so keep the book handy for future reference. But don't put off getting started. Your crawling baby will be a toddler before you know it.

CHAPTER SEVEN

Toddlers: Kids Who Are Walking

W<small>E HAD BEEN LOOKING AT HOMES FOR MONTHS.</small> We were expecting our second child, and although we could have fit everyone into our cramped two bedroom house, its location on a busy street made it less than suitable for a growing family.

Dick wanted more land in a less populated area. I wanted sidewalks and a location close to a neighborhood school and park. Dick was looking at foundations, landscaping, and plumbing. I was looking at nurseries and built-in dishwashers. Our real estate agent began to despair of ever finding something we could agree on.

But it was a family room that finally sold each of us on the same home. We both had imagined just such a room where our kids could spread out all of their toys and books, where there was more than enough storage and bookshelves for their belongings, and where there was room enough for three or four children to play together.

I laugh today when I consider how naive I was. There is never "enough" room for all of the stuff that children accumulate over the years. With the arrival of a second child and more toys and books, we soon outgrew those cupboards and bookshelves that had looked so spacious. I was always rearranging and reorganizing in a vain attempt to bring order out of chaos.

But don't be dismayed. The trappings of childhood that proliferate everywhere are the "stuff" of learning for children. I have learned to control my Dutch propensity for total cleanliness and order and have come to appreciate that clutter in our household is a sign of creativity, thinking, and accomplishment.

Just last week, Emily's bedroom floor was covered with books from the library, artwork in progress, dozens of letters from correspondents to be answered, and a jean jacket she was hand painting. Patrick's corner of the living room contained research materials for a junior seminar paper, rough drafts of articles for the school newspaper, back issues of the Chicago *Tribune*, and several old computer magazines.

Be warned that each new stage brings more "stuff" into your household. But soon that stuff will be replaced with silence and total cleanliness. This week Emily has returned to college, and her room is once again spotless. Patrick is off to the Soviet Union for a tour with a group of high school students. His projects were completed before he left. The clutter in the corner of the living room is gone. Enjoy it while you can!

In this chapter, you'll find suggestions for more toys, more books, and more arts and crafts materials. You'll find ideas for activities that create dust, confusion, and more than an occasional spilled mess. You'll be asked to sacrifice your sense of order and priorities. But the payoff will come in the form of interesting and vital children who will continually challenge you with their thinking and learning.

If the reality of life with a toddler has not yet hit you, then be prepared for exciting days ahead. Between his first birthday and the six months that follow, your precious darling will blossom into a real personality. If he isn't already walking, then very shortly he will begin to pull himself up and cruise along the furniture. Soon after that, he'll take off on his own and begin to actively explore every aspect of his environment. Childproof your house and let him go.

He'll begin saying words and phrases, if he isn't already. By the age of two, he will walk, run, get into everything, have an extensive vocabulary, and be learning new things at a prodigious rate. In the next few months your child will practice hammering, pounding, beating, touching, turning, looking, threading, opening, shutting, stacking, knocking down, picking up, twisting, turning, bouncing, rolling, retrieving, crayoning, creeping, crawling through, and dropping.

These months are "prime time" for learning. Don't let a day pass without stretching that little mind! Structure your home and activities so that you have to say "no" as little as possible.

Remember, the suggested activities that follow aren't designed to be done in any particular order. If an activity doesn't sound appealing to you, try something else. Children are permitted to have tastes and preferences also. They may not like the activity you have chosen. Choose another.

Please remember that each child develops on a different timetable. If an activity seems too difficult for your child, don't panic. He doesn't need a tutor or remedial classes. Children don't learn after just one exposure to a concept or skill. They need dozens of low-key opportunities to try. Never give your child the feeling that if he can't do it, you are frustrated or upset with him. Remember, this is not high pressure . . . you're supposed to be having fun!

THE TOY BOX

Just because your child has suddenly reached the magic age of one year doesn't mean you'll need to discard all of his baby toys and rush out to buy new ones. Most of the toys that entertained your infant in his first year will continue to be used well into the second. Your toddler may find different uses for them or play with them in more sophisticated ways, so don't be bound by the age recommendations on the packages.

In Chapter 6, all of my toy recommendations were generic. In this chapter, I will occasionally recommend a specific brand-name toy because of its unique qualities. Once again, I remind you these are only suggestions. Don't succumb to feelings of guilt that you can't buy one of everything. Children don't need one of everything. And very often their favorite toys are the least expensive ones!

TOYS YOU CAN BUY

Blocks. We started with simple alphabet blocks that came with their own wooden wagon. I'm sure I must have had the same set when I was growing up, for just to stack them gave me a comforting feeling. Then we graduated to colored blocks of different shapes and sizes. Our final block investment is still with us today. These large, unfinished wood blocks made tall, sturdy structures and entertained our children well into their school years.

Don't expect sophisticated structures in the beginning. Children start by carrying blocks around and making simple horizontal or vertical structures before progressing to the symmetrical and decorative buildings that five and six year olds often make. Just supply the blocks. Your children will do the rest. And don't be dismayed by the vigor with which young children destroy their creations. "Build and crash" is just part of the process.

Push and pull toys. This is an important category for the beginning walker. Two of our favorites were the Melody Push Chime and the colorful Corn Popper, both from Fisher Price.

Toy cars and trucks. Patrick loved the Fisher Price plastic construction vehicles. They could run into walls and furniture without doing too much damage, and their moving parts provided lots of imaginative play.

Small houses and people. We started out with the Fisher Price Play Family House and over the years added a farm, a gas station, and several others. Before long the tiny people that populate these toys seem to develop personalities of their own. Your child may even give them names. These toys engender hours of imaginative play and last forever. I hope to hand ours down to grandchildren!

Balls. Balls are the most inexpensive and well used toys of toddlers, and there are dozens of simple games to play with them. Have one that bounces well outdoors (ping pong balls are wonderful), one that is safe for indoor throwing (like a Nerf ball), and one that rolls easily over carpeted floors. You can even throw in a football for variety. Toddlers enjoy its strange shape.

Indoor slide. This toy comes highly recommended by many child development specialists. We never purchased one, but my children often played on them at friends' houses.

Incidentally, your children will often enjoy toys when they visit others, but don't necessarily rush out and buy a duplicate yourself. Your children may not find it nearly as attractive when it's right in their own backyard.

Straddle toys. There are dozens of variations of riding toys. You surely won't need more than one or two, since they take up a great deal of space, but they develop coordination and help burn up excess energy.

Pretend toys. I consider a toy telephone and cash register absolute musts in the toy box. They will be used for years to come and will be the basis for imaginative play and language development.

Hammering and pounding toys. As much as I disliked the constant pounding that accompanies these toys, they do have a great deal of value. Toddlers have an inborn need to hammer. Better they should do it on a pounding toy than on your antiques.

Nesting, stacking, sorting toys. This type of toy is excellent for developing problem-solving abilities in children. Our favorites were a set of nesting barrels in different colors, the Tupperware Shape Ball, and the Rock-A-Stack by Fisher Price, which consists of a number of different sized and colored rings that fit over a pole anchored in a base. You don't need more than one of a kind, however, since many toddlers are still too active for such fine motor activities.

Jack-in-the-boxes. I cannot recommend the traditional Jack-in-the-box because it is too complicated for a child to manage on his own. But the Surprise Box by Kohner is a wonderful toy that was a favorite of my children. Five small jack-in-the-boxes pop up to reveal animal figures. Toddlers have to push a lever, rotate a telephone dial, and complete several other movements to release the figures.

Cart, buggy, or *wagon.* Toddlers have an insatiable need to fill and empty containers and to move things from one place to another. One or more of these vehicles will give them a means of doing both. If you're not fussy they can be used inside and out.

Puzzles. The Fisher Price puzzles with small knobs and handles are perfect for some toddlers. Each puzzle has a theme and, while they are fitting the pieces together, children can learn to categorize as well. Look for puzzles that have pieces that are shaped like objects, people, or animals.

Many children will be frustrated by or uninterested in puzzles at first. Don't force the issue, and above all don't confuse your child with irregularly shaped puzzle pieces or puzzles that are too challenging.

Stuffed animals and dolls. Our closet shelves are still stuffed with favorite animal friends, some like brand new. One even went away to college for a brief stay, until he discovered that higher education wasn't his cup of tea.

Every child needs a teddy bear. Our teddy bear was joined by Small Pig, Little Lamb, and Babe the Blue Ox. But before you take in every stray you see, remember that each toy you buy has to be given a loving home. Most likely your child will love his first teddy bear best.

Wooden beads. Stringing beads is a perfect activity for developing fine motor coordination, and the results make lovely jewelry for pretend mommies.

Blackboard/easel. We found the perfect combination of these two essentials in one toy. There was a rack for chalk and eraser on one side and places to hold jars of paint on the other.

Tub and water toys. Make sure you have a supply of inexpensive toys to play with in the tub or backyard wading pool (this is an absolute must in hot weather). Keep them in a plastic bucket or net container for easy access.

I found water to be the best plaything my children ever had. They were always happy and could play for extended periods in either the bathtub or the wading pool. Sometimes just a pail of water and a big paint brush to "paint" the concrete driveway gave me thirty minutes of uninterrupted thinking time.

Rocking horse. Some families swear by these, but somehow we never got around to buying one . . . I always thought they were ugly. Naturally it was one of the first toys my children wanted to use at someone else's house. They are good for very active children who need to burn off excess energy, but younger children need close supervision.

Sandbox. This was the only "toy" that precipitated a major argument between my husband and me. I thought a sandbox was essential to every child's upbringing, and he thought that it was dirty and unsanitary (too many cats in the neighborhood). We compromised, and the kids played in someone else's sandbox. Our marriage survived, and so did our children. If you do approve of sand play, be sure to have all of the accoutrements to make it fun: pails, shovels, and construction toys.

Child-sized rocking chair or stool. To the small child, everything we adults use looks so big. It's nice to have a piece of furniture that is scaled down to pint size, although it's not essential if you don't have lots of extra room.

Red wagon. I believe that everyone's childhood should include a red wagon. It's perfect for taking toddlers on walks, provides a place to load and unload outdoor toys, and will come in handy when you need quick transportation for your landscaping chores.

TOYS YOU ALREADY OWN

Boxes, boxes, boxes. Oatmeal boxes make wonderful drums. Empty milk cartons make great building blocks (be sure to wash them thoroughly). Empty plastic margarine containers, yogurt containers, and egg cartons can easily be filled with all kinds of treasures. Larger boxes make great hiding places.

Kitchen toys. Empty frozen orange juice cans or paper towel rolls are great for rolling. A paper shopping bag is perfect for filling, emptying, and carting around valuable "junk." Measuring cups and plastic freezer containers nest and stack. Pots and pans make wonderful musical instruments (if you can stand the clatter). An empty metal coffee percolator to take apart and put together is a challenging toy. How about an old wastebasket of discarded mail? Children are often more entranced with "real" toys than with expensive store-bought ones.

Household junk. Discarded greeting cards, an old alarm clock with an unbreakable face, or even an old mattress to jump on will provide imaginative play opportunities for your toddler. Think twice before throwing anything out. Save those old purses for the emptying and filling play that delights children. Old (and clean) plastic wastebaskets or clothes baskets make better toy boxes than anything you can purchase.

Radio, record player, cassette player. Continue to expose your child to both adult and children's music. Start to memorize favorites.

Busy box. As your child grows older, change the contents of the busy box you created during the first year. We called ours a "goodie box," and the children saved their best found treasures in this box. The trick to keeping toddlers entertained and interested is variety. Keep the goodie box for those times when you need to have an absorbed child while you make a telephone call.

Furniture. Toddlers love to push cushions around and stack them. They adore crawling on and off the ottoman. Somehow living room furniture has much more appeal than expensive toys at this age. They also love to look in full length mirrors.

YOUR CHILD'S LIBRARY

Your child will continue to enjoy the books you selected during his first year, but will be ready for more challenging material in the months ahead. He will love books that can be manipulated such as touch-me books, books with snaps and zippers, and scratch and sniff books. You won't be able to check this variety out of the library, so be careful that what you purchase is well made and sturdy.

Look for stories that relate to familiar objects and routines. Children love illustrations that need sound effects and encourage participation. Look for "predictable books" with phrases that involve much repetition. These are not only fun to read, but will encourage your child to remember the words. Christian books are marked with an asterisk.

GOOD NIGHT MOON (Margaret Brown, Harper & Row, 1947)—A perfect story for bedtime read-aloud. The rhyming words and delightful illustrations will help your child make the transition from busy activities to a quiet and restful bedtime.

THE RABBIT (John Burningham, Thomas Y. Crowell, 1975)—You'll want to read every one of John Burningham's books to your child during the first three years. Each one has soft drawings, simple but beautifully written text, and—best of all—an undeniable appeal to the younger child. *The Baby*, *The Friend*, *The Blanket*, and *The Snow* all contain the same little boy and show him solving problems common to young children.

1, 2, 3 TO THE ZOO (Eric Carle, Collins World, 1968)— Animals are a sure-fire subject for a counting book, and in Eric Carle's version they are part of a train going to the zoo. If your toddler is going to the zoo, be sure to read this counting book both before and after your trip. Buy one or two good counting books and check others out of the library.

MARGUERITE DE ANGELI'S BOOK OF NURSERY AND MOTHER GOOSE RHYMES (Marguerite deAngeli, Doubleday, 1954)—If you want another Mother Goose book besides the one mentioned in Chapter 6, this would make a good addition. With 376 rhymes included, this anthology is one of the largest. A Caldecott Honor Book, the soft delicate illustrations in pastels never overpower the rhymes.

A TO Z PICTURE BOOK (Gyo Fujikawa, Grossett & Dunlap, 1974)—Fujikawa is a magnificent artist. You could spend hours with this book and never see all he has created. Some letters of the alphabet are illustrated with a double-page spread in full color. Other letters are shown with black and white line drawings of many different objects.

Check out a variety of alphabet books before you decide on a special one to purchase for your home library.

DAVY GOES PLACES (Lois Lenski, Henry Z. Walck, Inc., 1961)—The Davy books are small enough for toddlers to hold and look at on their own. Simple illustrations and text tell of everyday happenings in a little boy's life. They were favorites of my children. Other titles are: *Davy Goes Places, Davy and His Dog, Big Little Davy, A Dog Came to School, Surprise for Davy,* and *Davy's Day.*

BROWN BEAR, BROWN BEAR, WHAT DO YOU SEE? (Bill Martin, Jr., Illustrated by Eric Carle, Holt, Rinehard and Winston, 1983)—This title combines all of the elements a successful book for the toddler needs—bright illustrations, simple text, and an elegant concept. You will find before long that your toddler has memorized the words and is "reading" with you. Brown bear, red bird, yellow duck, and blue horse will soon become bedtime regulars at your house. Martin has written many other "predictable" favorites.

THE THREE LITTLE KITTENS (Misha, Golden Press, 1942)—Little Golden Books have delighted several generations of children. They must be purchased selectively, but they offer an inexpensive read-aloud that children can handle and enjoy for years. The illustrations that accompany this version of the favorite nursery rhyme are charming. Other Golden Book favorites at our house were: *We Help Daddy*, *The Little Red Hen*, *Animal Counting Book*, and *Baby Animals*.

BEST WORD BOOK EVER (Richard Scarry, Western, 1963)—Tiny drawings and busy pages are Richard Scarry's trademark. Children of all ages never seem to tire of asking, "What's this?" With this book your child can learn dozens of new words as little fingers can point to more than 1400 different objects illustrated in full color. Other titles are: *What Do People Do All Day?*, *Richard Scarry's ABC Word Book*, and *Richard Scarry's Great Big Air Book*.

MY OWN SPECIAL BODY* (Christine Harder Tangvald, David C. Cook, 1985)—Part of the God Made Me Special Series (*I Can Talk to God*, *When I Am Sick*, *Me, Myself, and I*, *My Family Is Special*, *My Friends are Special*, *Oh, Yes! Oh, No!*, and *Good For Me*), these lightweight board books are designed to develop your child's awareness that he is a unique creation of God. Each book is written about a different child and the illustrations are charming.

GOD GIVES US COLORS* (Carolyn Owens, David C. Cook, 1990)—This is just one of many Little Butterfly Shape books. Their distinctive shape and board covers make them easy to read aloud and handle. And they're just the right size for toddlers to tote around. Although inexpensive, they are colorful and sturdy. Standard publishes a similar Christian series titled Happy Day Books. These are Christian counterparts to the Golden Books that you no doubt remember from your own childhood. Golden Books can still be purchased at your supermarket or local bookstore.

ARTS AND CRAFTS SUPPLIES
Once your child is ready for these materials, the fun will never end. But don't rush the process if you feel your child isn't ready (probably not until 18-24 months). There will be plenty of time later.

Playdough and clay. Let your child experiment using safe kitchen tools like the rolling pin and plastic silverware. Don't force him to conform to your idea of a work of art. Just let him have fun.

PLAY DOUGH

2 cups flour	3/4 cup salt
1/2 cup water	1 tablespoon salad oil
Food coloring	

Mix flour and salt in a large bowl. Add water and oil and knead until mixture is smooth, about ten minutes. Add food coloring and continue kneading to mix completely. Store in a plastic bag in the refrigerator, and use it within a few days. Beware of using dough that has been around for awhile; it can pick up bacteria.

BAKING CLAY

2 cups flour	1 cup salt
3/4 cup water	Food coloring

Mix and knead as above. Unlike the play dough, this baking clay becomes hard when cooked in a 300 degree oven for an hour or two, depending on the thickness of the object. Use it for making hand prints. Press out the clay into a thick circle, let your toddler push his hand into it, then bake.

Discarded mail and greeting cards. Don't throw away the junk mail that cascades from your mailbox on a daily basis. Toddlers can sort, color, and cut it. Save it for when you want to work at your desk to pay bills or write a letter—your toddler will feel grown-up as he works alongside you.

Catalogs, magazines, posters, and pictures. Your toddler can make his own book using cut up pictures pasted on newsprint.

Sticky labels. Toddlers love self-stick labels from the stationery store. Brightly colored circles or just plain white ones to scribble on will give them a pre-pasting experience.

Paints, brushes, crayons. Toddlers can begin working in different mediums under supervision after the age of two.

Before that you'll probably only get frustrated. Get a big paint shirt or plastic apron to minimize damage to good clothing.

Please don't suggest that your child draw something specific or try to figure out exactly what he has drawn. And above all, don't buy coloring books! If you're a brave soul who can tolerate a bit of a mess, try your own hand at finger painting.

FINGER PAINT RECIPE
3 tablespoons cornstarch
3 tablespoons cold water
1/2 teaspoon liquid detergent
1 cup boiling water

Combine the cornstarch and water to form a paste. Then stir in the boiling water. Stir until smooth. Add the liquid detergent and vegetable coloring or tempera paint to get the color you want. Cool and start to paint!

Junk. Continue to collect spools, aluminum tins, and different sized boxes. Bring them all out on a rainy afternoon and see what you can construct. You can glue them together or just stack them. Collect lots of little things to make collages or other creations (beads, buttons, acorns, felt, fabric, corks, ribbon, seeds, seashells, straws, pipe cleaners, wallpaper, colored cellophane, popsicle sticks, paper doilies, etc.)

PARENT RESOURCE BOOKS
Many of the resource books mentioned in Chapter 6 will continue to help you as your child grows. In addition, read the following (asterisks indicate Christian books):

TODDLERS AND PARENTS: A DECLARATION OF INDEPENDENCE (T. Berry Brazelton, Delacorte Press, 1984)—Brazelton does for toddlers what he did for infants. Unfortunately, my children were grown by the time he wrote this second book.

*DARE TO DISCIPLINE** (James Dobson, Tyndale, 1970)—Be sure to mix in a healthy portion of discipline with your learning environment for maximum results. Dr. Dobson's ideas are proven.

A HUG AND A KISS AND A KICK IN THE PANTS* (Kay Kuzma, David C. Cook Publishing Co., 1987)—Another excellent source of creative ways to discipline. Molding the child while encouraging a free spirit is Dr. Kuzma's specialty.

LANGUAGE AND CONCEPT DEVELOPMENT

Talking. You can't talk too much to your toddler. Although you should never use "baby talk," you will speak more clearly and simply than you do when speaking to adults, especially when your child is beginning to talk.

Talk to your children about what is going on around them, about things they can hear, see, and feel. Talk about your work, the day's events, the groceries you're putting in the basket, and the food you're preparing. Describe what your child is doing. Ask questions. Repeat the words your toddler uses. Elaborate on what he says and act as an interpreter so other people can understand what he is saying. In the beginning, you may be his only communication link with other adults.

Daily routines. Use the daily routines to introduce vocabulary and concepts. Talk about getting dressed, getting the mail, eating meals, going out, picking up. Make games out of these mundane events and not only will life with toddlers be more interesting and manageable, they'll be learning all the while. Remember to include reading aloud (a Bible story every day), saying your prayers, and saying "I love you" as important daily routines.

Nursery rhymes and games. Now's the time to add some new rhymes to your repertoire, but don't neglect the old favorites. Putting motions with the words is excellent for coordination and following directions, in addition to being just plain fun! Your toddler won't just listen, he'll begin to say them with you.

Finger plays are good "sponge" activities to fill a restless moment. If you would like to learn more than just those mentioned here, consult "Wee Sing Children's Songs and Fingerplays" (a record from Price/Stern/Sloan) or *Baby's First Finger Rhymes* by Maida Silverman (Grossett & Dunlap, 1987).

Your "grown-up" toddler will enjoy pretending he's a baby again when you recite this one together:

Here's a ball for baby, big and soft and round.
(Cup your hands to form a ball.)
Here is baby's hammer. Oh, how he can pound.
(Make two fists, hold one over the other, and make the upper one pound the lower one.)
Here is baby's trumpet! Root-toot-toot-toot-toot.
(Hold fist to mouth and pretend to play.)
Here's the way that baby plays at peek-a-boo.
(Cover your face with your hands and then uncover it.)
Here's the big umbrella, keep the baby dry.
(Curve one hand like an umbrella top, hold the other under it stiff like a handle.)
Here's the baby's cradle. Rock-a-baby-bye.
(Fold your arms and pretend to rock a baby.)

If you don't remember this one from your own childhood, it's not too late to learn it now (sing to the tune of "Frére Jacques"):

Where is Thumbkin? (Hold up one thumb.)
Where is Thumbkin? (Hold up other thumb.)
Here I am. (Wiggle one thumb.)
Here I am. (Wiggle other thumb.)
How are you today sir? (Wiggle one thumb.)
Very well, I thank you. (Wiggle other thumb.)
Run away. (Put one thumb behind your back.)
Run away. (Put other thumb behind your back.)

Other verses inquire, "Where is Tallman (or Middleman)?" "Where is Ringman?" and "Where is Pinky?" You can also extend this rhyme to other parts of the body, (e.g. "Where Is Elbow?" or "Where Is Ankle?").

I had not heard the following rhyme until I recently observed our kindergarten class having fun with it, but I know that toddlers will love it:

The wheels on the bus go round and round
(Form fists and circle them around each other.)
Round and round, round and round.

(Continue circling.)
The wheels on the bus go round and round
(Continue circling.)
All around the town.
(Take index finger and make a circle motion.)
Other verses:
The doors on the bus go open and shut . . .
(Put hands together in a prayer position and then
open and shut them, keeping your thumbs touching.)
The windows on the bus go up and down . . .
(Move hands up and down as if opening a window.)
The wipers on the bus go swish, swish, swish . . .
(With thumbs together, point your index fingers and
waggle them side-to-side like windshield wipers.)
The driver on the bus says "Move on back . . ."
(Make a hitchhiking motion.)
The babies on the bus go "Wah! Wah! Wah!"
(Rub your eyes and pretend to cry.)
The mommies on the bus go "Sh! Sh! Sh!"
(Put index finger in front of mouth.)

Following directions. Play a variation of Simon Says called "Mommy Says." This game will give your toddler an opportunity to learn to follow simple directions. Demonstrate the action while giving the directions. Say: "Mommy says put your hand on your head." When your child has followed the direction, go on to another. Say, "Mommy says put your hands on your knees." "Mommy says touch your toes three times."

READING AND READING READINESS

Reading aloud. You should now be reading on a daily basis to your toddler. If he is ready for a story and asks for one, be prepared to drop what you're doing and respond. But don't force a child to sit and listen when he is scrambling off your lap. Five or six minutes of quiet reading will be the maximum in the beginning As children's attention spans increase and their interests mature, you can stretch this time. Be prepared, however, for those children who will listen to as many stories at bedtime as you are willing to read.

Book talk. In addition to reading books aloud, there are many other short activities that prepare a child for being a good reader. Name the pictures; make silly sounds (fire engines, animals, cars, and trucks); find a character or object that recurs on page after page; find the hidden pictures; play hide and seek (where's the bunny? or where's the kitten?); or retell the story in different words; purposefully make a mistake in labeling or in telling the story and see if your child figures it out.

Homemade books. If you and your child both have the time and patience, make your own books together. Make one of greeting cards you get from relatives. Make an "All About Me" book with pictures of your child. Make an animal or zoo book with pictures from old copies of *National Geographic* or *Ranger Rick* magazines. Make books for shopping—one for the grocery store, one for the hardware store, or wherever else you like to shop together.

Library trips. Make weekly trips to the library to check out books and records. You'll want to buy copies of favorites, but don't limit your child's reading simply to the books you own. Borrow as many as you have time to read and more.

Book shopping trips. If your budget permits, go shopping for an inexpensive book at the supermarket or discount store. Our local stationery store has a wonderful revolving rack of sized down Golden Books, and our Christian bookstore offers similar choices by David C. Cook and Standard.

VALUES

Manners. Josh Billings says, "Train up a child in the way he should go, and walk there yourself once in awhile." Children must see good manners, politeness, and caring modeled on a daily basis. They do not turn into ladies and gentlemen overnight, but neither can you suddenly decide, after neglecting manners for five years, that you will teach your child to be polite and share his toys before he starts school in September.

Following rules. Make your rules short and simple; don't overdo limit setting. We found that child-proofing our home for a short time was much easier than setting totally unreasonable limits that made life miserable for both parents and child. Use distraction. Reinforce desirable behavior and ignore undesirable behavior. One author suggests rhyming rules that are easy to remember:

If you hit, you must sit.

Put your dinner in your tummy
And you will get a snack that's yummy.

Toys left out make parents sad.
Toys picked up make parents glad.

Stories to teach values. There are many outstanding books that do an excellent job of imparting values. Books such as the following ones help children develop Christian character and biblical values: *My Friends Are Special* (A book about relationships from the "God Made Me Special" series by Christine Harder Tangvald, Illustrated by June Goldsborough, David C. Cook Publishing, 1987); *Too Many Bunnies* (A book about friendliness from the "Brenda Learns about God" series by Elspeth Campbell Murphy, Illustrated by Anne Kennedy, David C. Cook Publishing, 1987); and *Leif Cleans His Room* (A book about responsibility from the "My Friend Leif" series, David C. Cook Publishing, 1986).

Prayer and Bible reading. Read a Bible story every day. Pray before each bedtime. Choose stories that appeal to your children and say prayers that are simple and meaningful to them.

PHYSICAL DEVELOPMENT AND PLAY ACTIVITIES

I hope you haven't forgotten our very important discussion in an earlier chapter about the value of play to your children's intellectual development. The period between twelve and thirty months is a crucial one. The foundations of intelligence are being laid and play is the mortar that holds the bricks together.

A great share of the time you will merely provide the materials and environment in which play will occur, but there are many occasions in which you will structure simple games and join in the play with your child. Children love repetition. Just doing a game or activity once is never enough.

Exercises. Shortly after Patrick was born, I began a series of exercises designed to put my body back into shape. I found that Emily delighted in joining me. We did the exercises to music and, although she frequently got in my way, she thoroughly enjoyed the workout. If you would like to develop a regular workout for your child, consult *How to Keep Your Child Fit from Birth to Six* by Bonnie Prudden (Harper & Row, 1964).

Games. "Go-between" needs two people (preferably Mom and Dad) who sit on the floor a few feet apart and send their toddler back and forth between them. Naturally junior will stop for hugs and kisses after each crossing.

"Messenger Service" also keeps your active toddler on the move. Give him socks to take to the bedroom or towels to put in the kitchen drawer. He can even deliver dad's slippers to him, if dads wear slippers anymore.

"Chase" is an ever popular game, preferably not played before bedtime (which is when most fathers like to play it). Get down on all fours and try to escape from your eager toddler.

Catch. Between the ages of one and two, children can begin playing a true game of catch. At first the adult can bounce or roll the ball and the child will simply fetch it. Then the toddler can toss the ball to the adult who is standing up close who will catch it and hand it back to the child. Rolling the ball back and forth between two seated people is also a good way to get the idea. Your child will show you when he's ready to both throw and catch the ball. Dads who are former baseball and football stars are always a little anxious about waiting, but encourage them to be patient.

Cornmeal, oatmeal, or *rice sandbox.* If it's too cold to play outside in the sandbox, create your own from one of kitchen staples. My preference is rice. Gather funnels, muffin tins, sieve, measuring spoons and cups, empty margarine and yogurt containers, and small cars and trucks (if age appropriate). Fill a large rectangular box that has been trimmed to about six inches in height and fill with your "sand." When play is over, save the "sand" for another rainy day.

Sandbox. Although you can purchase or make elaborate sandboxes, an inexpensive one can be made by filling a plastic wading pool with clean sand from the garden center. Just remember to cover it at night to keep out rain and animals.

Outside fun with water. Water play is wonderful. Wash rocks, paint the sidewalk, wash bikes or Big Wheels, fill lots of small empty containers from a wading pool or pail, or just run under the sprinkler.

If you have the room, spread a heavy plastic dropcloth over a grassy area. Turn on the sprinkler and you'll create a super water slide. Supervise carefully and make sure you keep the sprinkler running. Don't forget to move the plastic dropcloth when you're finished. You could end up planting new grass if the day is hot.

Inside fun with water. Write with soap based crayons on the tile and wash it off with sponges. I never tried this, but it sounds like fun. Make sure your children don't think that you can write on the living room walls with crayons as well.

Even if you don't attempt bathroom art, be sure you have plenty of containers and toys for bathtub fun. Ideas for water play toys: tea strainer, plastic measuring cup and spoons, clear flexible tubing, eye dropper, plastic boats and blocks, squeeze bottles, plastic container with holes punched in sides, and sponges of different varieties and sizes.

Obstacle course. Of course you've seen the wonderful obstacle courses in outdoor playgrounds. You can create your own in the play room with a pile of pillows to climb over, an indoor slide if you have one, a kitchen chair to crawl under, and a tunnel. You can make the tunnel by cutting out two sides of a large cardboard box or spreading a blanket over a card table.

Balloon play. Batting balloons is wonderful fun. Save this game for when you acquire a new balloon from the shoe store or a local carnival. Show your toddler how to keep the balloon aloft and then let him try. Or, sit on the floor and bat it back and forth.

Touching games. Give your toddler lots of opportunities to touch interesting things. So much of the time we are saying "Don't touch!" Do this informally, but make sure you do it! If you're ambitious, make a "Touching Book" with samples of fabric (cotton, burlap, corduroy, velvet, dotted swiss, denim, wool, terry cloth), sandpaper of various textures, wallpaper samples, and old greeting cards with glitter or embossed surfaces.

Fill and dump games. Toddlers never tire of this activity, and there are many variations on it. Clip colored clothespins around the edge of a coffee can and take turns dropping them inside. They make a wonderful sound as they fall. Or make an opening in the plastic top of an empty coffee can and show your child how to drop jar lids into the opening. (Remember, whenever you use a coffee can for a toy, make sure the sharp edges have been hammered smooth or covered with heavy duty tape.)

Rolling games. Show your child how to roll miniature cars down a ramp. Prop up a sturdy piece of cardboard or lumber and watch the toys roll down. A large mailing tube also makes a great place to roll miniature toys.

Paper play. This inexpensive form of play you used with your crawling baby is also perfect for toddlers. You can use pages from old magazines, discarded telephone books, waxed paper (this was my favorite for keeping my toddler amused while I was making dinner), tissue from clothing boxes, mail advertisements. Squeeze it, crumple it, throw it. Just don't eat it.

MUSIC

Songs. In addition to the finger plays set to music that we learned earlier, introduce your child to some old favorites by buying or borrowing records from your public library. Hap Palmer, Ella Jenkins, and Pete Seeger are favorite performers for children. Some excellent records include *The Mr. Rogers*

Neighborhood Series; *Peter, Paul, and Mommy* by Peter, Paul, and Mary (Warner Brothers); and the *Wee Sing* Series (Price/Stern/Sloan).

Make sure your children hear "Farmer in the Dell," "Three Blind Mice," "Mary Had a Little Lamb," "Row, Row, Row, Your Boat," "Ten Little Indians," "Paw Paw Patch," "Old MacDonald Had a Farm," "Skip to My Lou," "Are You Sleeping?" "This Old Man," "The Bear Went Over the Mountain," "My Bonnie Lies over the Ocean," "Jimmy Crack Corn," "Yankee Doodle," "Down by the Station," "I'm a Little Teapot," "Here We Go Round the Mulberry Bush," and "Ring Around the Rosie."

For words, music, and more songs consult *American Folk Songs for Children* by Ruth Crawford Seeger (Doubleday & Co., 1953), *Tom Glazer's Treasury of Songs for Children* by Tom Glazer (Doubleday, 1988), and *Jim Along, Josie*, by Nancy and John Langstaff (Harcourt, Brace, Jovanovich, 1970).

Homemade musical instruments. Here are some wonderful musical instruments to make out of simple materials.

Sandpaper blocks: Using glue, cover two 2″ x 4″ x 1″ blocks of wood with sandpaper. If you're especially clever, add a knob to the back of each. They make a wonderful swishing sound when rubbed together.

Bells: Sew bells on a band of elastic that your child can wear on his wrist or ankle. When your child moves, the bells will ring. See if you can get him to move his arm or leg in time to music you sing or play.

Tambourine: Attach bells to the edge of a paper or foil pie plate with a twist tie. Shake the tambourine in time to music.

Maracas: Fill empty film cannisters with different kinds of dried food—peas, beans, or rice. Glue the tops securely and experiment with different combinations of sounds.

Rhythm sticks: Buy a couple of wooden dowels at the hardware store or lumber yard and you'll have your own set of rhythm sticks. If you can locate a fluted stick, rub the smooth one over it to create a different rhythm sound.

COOKING AND HOUSEHOLD FUN

In the following section, you'll find some recipes that are easy enough for the 18- to 30-month-old toddler to help you make. Just beware that the making may be more fun than the eating. There is no accounting for the food preferences of toddlers. So don't be upset if after the extensive preparation, you are the only one eating your creation!

CRUNCHY PUDDING

1 cup applesauce	1 cup vanilla yogurt
1/3 cup raisins	3/4 cup Grape Nuts Flakes

Chill applesauce and yogurt so the pudding will be ready to eat immediately after mixing the ingredients. Mix applesauce and yogurt together. Add Grape Nuts Flakes and raisins. Stir gently and serve. Will serve 4 to 5 children's portions.

ENGLISH MUFFIN PIZZA

English muffins	Mozzarella cheese
Pizza or spaghetti sauce	

Split the English muffins in half with a dull knife. Cut the mozzarella cheese into bite sized pieces and put the pizza sauce in a bowl. Give children a knife, spoon, and cutting board. Cut the cheese into even smaller pieces. Spoon sauce onto English muffin. Place the small pieces of cheese on top of the sauce. Heat in toaster oven or microwave until cheese melts. When cool, cut into quarters.

FROZEN BANANAS

1 cup apple juice	1/2 banana per serving
1 cup unsweetened coconut	
1 cup toasted wheat germ	

Set up separate bowls of wheat germ, coconut, and apple juice. Give children half of a banana and have them insert a popsicle stick into it. Holding a popsicle stick, show them how to dip the banana in the apple juice, then in the wheat germ or coconut. Wrap the banana pops in tinfoil and freeze overnight.

FRUIT MILKSHAKES

1/2 quart milk   2 bananas
5-6 strawberries   5-6 ice cubes
2-3 tablespoons honey

Pour milk into blender. Cut the bananas into a few pieces using a dull knife. Add to blender. Have children cut tops off strawberries. Add strawberries to the blender. Add the ice cubes and blend for a few minutes.

PEANUT BUTTER SESAME BALLS

2 tablespoons nonfat dry milk
1/2 tablespoon toasted wheat germ
1/4 cup coconut   2 tablespoons honey
1/2 cup peanut butter 1 cup sesame seeds (hulled)

Mix dry ingredients together (except sesame seeds). Add to the peanut butter and honey. Give children a large piece of the mixture to form into a ball. Put sesame seeds in a plate and have children roll their peanut butter balls in the seeds.

PEANUT BUTTER, JELLY, AND CREAM CHEESE SANDWICHES

Peanut butter   Jelly
Cream cheese   Bread (firm)

Put all ingredients in separate bowls. Cut the bread slices in half. Make sandwiches.

ARTS, CRAFTS, AND CREATIVITY

Sticker fun. Save those wildlife stickers, Easter and Christmas seals, and the self-adhesive dots that come in so many wonderful shapes and sizes from the stationery store. Toddlers can make a simple collage with little supervision.

Masking tape fun. If I could buy only one thing from the hardware store to entertain children, it would be masking tape. Toddlers can create tape pictures, stick the tape on themselves and their clothes, even make pretend highways on tile floors for their cars and trucks.

If you want to create a "formal" art project, buy some construction paper and several different kinds of tape (colored Mystick tape or masking tape). Cut lengths of tape and attach them to the edge of the tabletop. Create a picture on the construction paper with the tape.

Deodorant bottle markers. When you've run out of roll-on deodorant, rinse out the bottle and fill it with thinned finger paint. Voila! You have a giant marker.

Collages. You can glue anything to a piece of construction paper, poster board, or heavy cardboard, and you'll have a collage: torn construction paper, torn newspaper or comics, leaves of various shapes and sizes, beans, rice, seed pods, bark, small twigs, nuts, bolts, feathers, toothpicks, or popsicle sticks. Clean out your junk and sewing drawers every now and then and turn the kids loose with Elmer's. If you put the makings of the collage in a paper bag, you can call it a "Surprise Collage."

Necklaces. Cut cardboard tubes from paper towels and toilet paper into rings of varying lengths. You'll need about ten rings for a good necklace. Paint them first if you want a colorful necklace. Knot the rope, slip an index card up to the knotted end to keep the tubes from falling off. Thread the tubes, tear off the index card and tie the ends together. Supervise the wearing of this necklace so that it won't get twisted or pulled too hard.

Q-tip painting. All you'll need is food coloring in a paint pan and some white paper. This is easier than using brushes because you can just throw the Q-tips away when you're done. Try some color mixing magic. Yellow and blue make green, remember!

Sponge painting. Tiny pieces of sponge also make a great substitute for paint brushes. Discard them when finished.

Snowy day picture. Use black paper and white chalk. You can make a snowstorm or a snowman.

Finger painting. You can use the recipe given earlier in the chapter. Remember to use glossy paper (shiny shelf paper or special finger paint paper sold at the art store). Wet it down with a damp sponge, add a little paint, demonstrate, and your toddler is off.

MATH AND SCIENCE

Growing carrot tops. Cut off the tops of some carrots and put them in a saucer. Surround them with small stones to keep them in place. Always keep a little water in the dish. Wait a week and see what happens. Keep in mind that everything you plant won't always grow. But don't be discouraged. Try again.

Growing fruit seeds. Collect seeds from oranges, lemons, apples, grapefruit, or pumpkins. Let the seeds dry for several hours. Put some soil in paper cups, egg cartons, or glass jars. Plant the seeds near the top. Let your toddler water them each day and watch them grow

Growing kidney beans. Soak them overnight in water and they will sprout faster. You can place them between a layer of damp paper towel and the inside of the glass jar. Keep the paper towel moist and they'll have enough light and water to sprout. Once you have two inches of growth, move the sprouts to paper cups full of soil for further growth. Don't forget to water and place in full light.

Growing sweet potatoes. Immerse the pointed end of a sweet potato in a glass jar filled with water. You won't want to rest the potato on the bottom of the jar, so stick some toothpicks in the potato to keep it resting on the jar's rim. When the potato grows, it will send out roots into the water and leaves on top. After about two weeks you can plant them in pots, or with warm weather, outside. Or, you can throw it out and do something else. You aren't obligated to keep everything you start growing!

Flowers, trees, and shrubs. Our earliest field trips were to Cantigny, a beautiful museum-estate with formal gardens. Emily's first word was *flower*, and after that we just kept adding the names of all the trees and shrubs we saw. On your walks outside, watch for signs of the seasons. Talk about the differences between evergreen and deciduous trees.

Ice cube fun. Put two or three ice cubes in a bowl. Compare them to water. Melt them on the stove. Pour them back into the ice cube tray and refreeze. Talk about it as you go.

You can get as technical as you want. Toddlers are fascinated by this process and you never know what they are learning.

Bathtub fun. Talk about the difference between sinking and floating. Try these objects and see what happens: a wooden spoon, a bar of Ivory soap, a cork, a teething ring, a wooden block, a rubber ball, and a wooden toothpick. Then try these: a house key, a large stone, a paper clip, and a metal button. Fun, isn't it?

Air experiments. If it's summertime, use your fan to try out a windmill or a pinwheel. Tie ribbons to the fan and watch the way they blow.

Weather. Collect some snow in a container. Bring it in the house and come back later to see what has happened. Take it outside again and watch it freeze. Talk about the wind. Notice how it sounds and what it does to the trees and leaves on the ground. Get a big calendar and draw pictures on it everyday to tell about the weather.

Math concepts. Keep playing the same games we introduced in Chapter 6. Who is taller? Which is longer? Which holds more? Which is heavier? Continue to count and talk about numbers. Constant exposure to concrete examples will give your children a "real" understanding of mathematics and not just the ability to deal with numbers in a rote way.

FIELD TRIPS

The field trips mentioned in Chapter 6 continue to be good ones for toddlers, but consider adding some new locations also. Try to find some read-alouds that correlate with your field trips. They can set the stage for the trip and help your children relive it once it's over.

Pet store. Make sure your young ones know you aren't doing any serious shopping (unless you are). My kids always wanted to bring home several different varieties of tropical fish. Read *The Pet Show* by Ezra Jack Keats (Collier/Macmillan, 1972).

Fire station. Our local fire department plans special activities each year for fire prevention week. There are opportunities to ride in an engine and tour the fire house. See if your community offers the same. If not, suggest it. There are several good books to read before and after your visit: *The Fire Cat* by Esther Averill (Harper, 1983), *Curious George at the Fire Station* by Margaret and H.A. Rey (Houghton Mifflin, 1985), and *Fireman Critter* by Mercer Mayer (Simon & Schuster, 1986).

Parent's work place. No matter where you work, it's fun to give your child an idea of how you spend all of that time away from home. Make the visit short and feature the most exciting parts of the job (like the cafeteria with a pop machine or the desk with lots of different colored markers). Richard Scarry's book, *Busy Workers* (Golden Book, 1987), will introduce your child to many different occupations.

Ride on the bus or train. We live near a suburban rail line, so Emily and I took a short train ride several stops down the line, where Dad met us and took us out for ice cream. We saw just enough out the window to keep us intrigued, got our tickets punched by the conductor, and had a chance to hear him call out the names of neighboring towns.

Construction site. If you live in an area where new construction is going up, trucks, machinery, and construction workers are always fascinating to toddlers. Just make sure you keep a safe distance away. Read *Curious George and the Dump Truck* by Margaret and H.A. Rey (Houghton Mifflin, 1984) and *The Big Book of Real Trucks* by George Zaffo (Grossett and Dunlap, 1976).

Creating a learning environment for your child between the ages of twelve and thirty months is more challenging than it was during your child's first year. Your eager learner will begin to exert his own personality and preferences. Now, he can move about on his own and doesn't stay in one location. You'll need more stamina, more patience, and more creativity! Keep this volume at hand for easy reference.

CHAPTER EIGHT

Preschoolers: Kids Who Are Talking

IN PREPARATION FOR WRITING THIS CHAPTER, I took a little walk down Memory Lane. I got out the baby books and browsed through the pages of milestones and memories. I leafed through the photo albums with shots of smiling preschoolers playing on playground equipment, running through sprinklers, riding carousels, opening Christmas presents, and burying themselves in autumn leaves. But the most fun of all was digging through the art boxes.

Since both of my children have always been pack rats, and I couldn't convince them to part with their artistic creations, the next best alternative was getting everything organized. We covered cardboard storage containers with brightly colored Contac paper, and into these boxes went the carefully constructed macaroni and seed collages, the pictures made with sequins, popsicle sticks, toothpicks, and cotton balls. As I browsed through them, I recognized fabric from my old slipcovers and a worn cotton bathrobe. In my daughter's imagination they had become the perfect beard for a face she'd created.

Perhaps when more time and space separates them from home, my teenagers will be willing to part with these precious creations. But for now, I'm glad they saw fit to keep them. The faded construction paper and fabric remnants have once again reminded me of how important the little things are to children. They also brought to mind how quickly my children grew and changed in the years between two-and-a-half and five. Each day, it seemed, they learned a new skill or piece of information.

Creating a learning environment for your children of these ages is much more demanding. Your preschoolers have no doubt developed real minds of their own and personalities to match. They have an insatiable need to know "why" and expect you to come up with all of the right answers. They are capable of doing all kinds of interesting things and being most helpful and independent, while at the same time dissolving into tears if they cannot learn to tie their shoes *today*. But you'll be delighted at the fun you can have with your preschoolers.

In this chapter you'll find dozens of ideas and activities to help your children learn. Again I'll remind you that you won't be able to do them all, you needn't do them in any particular order, and they aren't meant to be done on a daily basis. Some will become part of your routine, especially reading aloud and language and concept development. Others will be perfect for that moment when you need something special. Experiment, adapt, and enjoy.

THE TOY BOX

You will find that most of the toys purchased for your children in earlier stages will continue to be used. Every now and then, put a few toys away for a week or two. When you bring them out again, they will seem fresh and new. Too many toys or too much clutter will often confuse children.

TOYS YOU CAN BUY

Tricycle. Many over-anxious parents (the McEwans, for example) purchase a tricycle for their child far in advance of his ability to use it. Postponing the purchase until children are really ready will be a happier experience for everyone. You don't need an expensive trike. We bought one from a friend. No doubt because I never had any concrete surfaces on which to ride my trike or bike (we lived in the country and everything was gravel), I derived much satisfaction watching my daughter pedal her tricycle up and down the driveway and sidewalk. I probably enjoyed it more than she did.

Small table or desk. We bought an old school desk and chair at a sale and kept it in the garage. It was perfect for doing messy art projects on the patio or driveway. We could have used another one inside, but used the dining room table instead.

Bulletin board. Once your children start creating art, be sure you have a place to display all of the treasures. The refrigerator is also a good place to attach things with magnets.

Housekeeping toys. It's easy to get carried away in buying housekeeping toys. You can get stoves and sinks that actually work. I preferred using the real stove and sink and investing our toy dollars elsewhere. We did buy lots of pretend food, some toy dishes, and plenty of dolls to attend tea parties. You can also buy toy brooms, carpet sweepers, etc.

Garden toys. Since I enjoy gardening and yard work more than housekeeping, we bought a play lawnmower, wheelbarrow, shovels, hoes, and cultivating tools. I always had plenty of help when I was weeding.

Construction sets. These are essential for all preschoolers. We began with the Lego Preschool Set and then graduated to more complex sets. I could count on at least an hour when Patrick got engrossed in building with his Legos. As he got older, he built entire towns. My only problem was in convincing him to disassemble his creations—he thought we should just buy more Legos!

We also purchased some of the pre-designed kits that created trucks, planes, and complicated buildings. An old-fashioned construction set that really got a workout at our house was Lincoln Logs. (I suspect it was because Dad loved to build with them on nights that he was baby-sitting.) Also excellent are the old-fashioned Tinker-Toys.

Puzzles. The Lauri Company makes outstanding puzzles from crepe foam rubber. They come in a variety of subjects but especially good are the ones for numbers, letters (both lower and upper case), and shapes. (Lauri also makes nifty little construction sets from the same crepe foam and small wooden pegs. They might be a little difficult for preschoolers, but with help they can manage.) Wooden puzzles by Playskool are also excellent.

Alphabets. Learning the alphabet is the first step in learning to read. Parents are understandably proud when their offspring can recite it, but give your children lots of opportunities to experience the letters in other ways as well.

In addition to the alphabet blocks you purchased earlier and the puzzles mentioned above, buy some inexpensive cardboard stencils and a set of magnetic letters and/or wooden letters. You won't need to give formal lessons; let your children play with them.

Wall maps of the United States and world, and a globe. It's not too early to begin giving your children an awareness of geography. *National Geographic* publishes some excellent large maps. If you're really adventuresome, they make wonderful wallpaper.

Big Wheels. When first I heard these noisy contraptions, I vowed that no child of mine would ever pollute the air waves. Naturally, I gave in and purchased a Big Wheel, but somehow we never got around to attaching the noise maker. My children always wondered why their Big Wheels were so quiet.

I can't tell you how much fun my kids had with them. They not only rode them, they built on them, turned them upside down and fixed them, gave their dolls and animals rides in them, had races with each other, and much more. I gave them to a friend with younger children, and my teenagers still lament their passing.

Play people and objects. We continued to add to our collection of Fisher Price Play People and discovered the Playmobil series as well. Preschoolers can engage in all kinds of imaginative play with these toys.

We collected the hospital set, the cowboy set, and—a total extravagance—the pirate set. My daughter has such fond memories of the Playmobils that she recently purchased a key ring with a Playmobil figure dressed as a London bobby.

Miniature animals. Over the years we managed to collect sets of very small farm and zoo animals, as well as assorted dinosaurs. These came in very handy for all sorts of pretend games, and they were also great for building dioramas once the children were in school.

Expensive dollhouses and train sets. These are usually given to children by mothers and fathers who really want the toys for themselves. Consequently, parents are never happy with how their children play with them. If you can let go of your gift and allow your children to play with it the way they want to, then go ahead and make the investment. Otherwise, why pretend—just buy it for yourself!

Blocks, beads, pattern cards, pegboards and play tiles. Make sure you have some of each of these toys. They are great for making designs and patterns, learning geometric shapes, and using fine motor muscles. Some sets like Playtiles from Playskool and Mr. Mighty Mind and Mr. Super Mind come with activity cards containing patterns of varying difficulty. These are good reading readiness activities.

Rhythm instruments. If you didn't make your own from Chapter 6, consider doing it now, or purchase some inexpensive ones. Preschoolers love making music.

Arts and crafts kits. If you're uncertain about just what art materials to buy, why not start with a kit that's been assembled for you? Crayola has a kit that I purchased for both of my children. They liked the convenient rack that held lots of different crayons and markers. Fisher-Price also makes a set with watercolors, safety scissors, ruler, chalk, crayons, construction paper, and an idea booklet.

Lotto games. These inexpensive games are excellent for memory, reading readiness, and vocabulary development. Edu-Cards has six different sets (ABC, Zoo, Farm, World Around Us, What's Missing, Go Together Lotto, and Object Lotto).

Inexpensive toys that every child should have once in a lifetime. Kites, kaleidoscopes, yo-yos, balsa wood airplanes, hand puppets, bubble pipes, Frisbees, Old Maid games, and a variety of multicolored bouncing balls all fall into this category. I'm sure there are others. These are the toys that you pick up on a trip to the drugstore or dimestore. They don't cost much and probably won't last long, but your children will have a short period of very intense fun with them. Once in a while it's okay to give in to their requests!

Junk toys you swore you'd never buy. Included in this category are the vast array of cereal premiums that you will send away for until your child realizes that reality never matches the picture on the box. These lessons are too valuable to skip. My editor tells how her six-year-old saved her allowance for weeks so she could purchase a crystal growing set at the grocery store. This four-dollar expenditure seemed like a waste to the mom, but she wisely let her daughter indulge her curiosity.

Transportation toys. Trucks, cars, fire engines, and construction equipment of all kinds continue to be popular for pretend play for both boys and girls. We always avoided the very popular Tonka trucks, because I selfishly enjoyed having finish on my furniture and paint on my walls. We purchased items in plastic and found them to be less damaging.

Dolls and stuffed animals. These familiar members of the family will attend tea parties, ride in wagons and buggies, and accompany children as they play. Follow your children's taste in selecting an occasional addition to the family.

Thinking my daughter would love to dress her doll with homemade clothes, I labored for several months to create a custom wardrobe for a favorite doll. Emily looked at the clothes once and preferred to keep the doll in the dress she arrived in. My feelings were only hurt for a little while. (Maybe her daughter will enjoy my handiwork.)

TOYS YOU ALREADY OWN

Budding young mechanic's box. Find a sturdy box and fill it with a screwdriver, springs, padlocks and keys, old clocks to take apart, radio parts, pulleys, bits of rope, latches, wheels, basin plugs, door stoppers, zippers, short chains, bunches of keys, marbles, doorknobs, nuts and bolts, and paper clips.

Budding young artist's box. Find a sturdy box and fill it with pictures from magazines of food, cars, trains, and planes, old greeting cards, postcards, bank deposit slips, transfers, coupons, empty stamp books, paper lace doilies, bits of cellophane and foil, strips of colored paper, and colored straws.

Budding young puppet maker's box. Find a sturdy box and fill it with round wooden clothespins, crayons to make faces, bits of wool to glue as hair, and all kinds of fabric scraps to make costumes.

Budding young author's box. Find a sturdy box and fill it with small note pads, sharpened pencils, a small stapler, a hole punch, a paperback dictionary, and crayons to draw illustrations.

Paper pile. Collect paper of every conceivable size and variety. Examples are: wallpaper books, printers' remnants (call your local printer and see what he has available), white butcher's paper, newsprint available in art stores, brown paper grocery bags (never get plastic), shirt cardboards, shelf paper, paper plates, and construction paper.

Picture pile. Save old magazines, junk mail, old catalogs, greeting cards, and fronts of food boxes.

Button box. I still remember my grandmother's button box. It was a treasure trove of interesting buttons, and she could tell stories about where many of them came from. Don't ever throw a button away.

Sheets and blankets. Always have some spare sheets and blankets that you no longer use for bedding. They make wonderful costumes, tents, wigwams, or dropcloths for messy projects. Toss one over a small table and—presto— you have a pirate's cave, a castle, or a secret hideout. Add a flashlight for even more fun.

Shell box. Save those shells for sorting, gluing, or just plain looking.

Let's pretend boxes. These boxes contain the props that will help your children take on new identities. You can make them as elaborate or simple as you wish.

Auto mechanic—Flashlight, keys on a big ring, simple tools and a visored hat.

Barber/beautician—Brush, comb, curlers, shaving brush, old shirt for uniform, plastic scissors (make sure they won't really cut hair).

Doctor/nurse—Stethoscope made from a spool wrapped in foil and tied onto a string, clean rags for slings and bandages, cotton balls, eye dropper, tongue depressors, plastic squeeze bottle with water, prescription pad, toy hypodermic needle (you can pick up some of these props during a routine visit to the doctor).

Police officer or firefighter—Wear a badge made of foil over cardboard. Tape a safety pin on the back. Pick up an inexpensive fire hat and add a whistle or piece of hose depending on the role.

Grocery store—Play money, toy cash register, food packages, and a pretend shopping cart if you have one.

Fairy princess—Crown made of colored paper or foil, stick for a wand wrapped in foil with a star glued on top, mother's old prom dress.

Post office—Gummed lables or Easter seals for stamps, envelopes, junk mail, grocery bags and tape to make packages, stamp pad and rubber stamp, shoulder bag to deliver mail.

Pirate—Bandana to tie around head, patch for the eye, and a pirate earring (a loop of thread through a large, shiny, button), a cardboard sword covered with foil, and a telescope made from a paper towel tube.

Indian brave—Feathers cut from construction paper glued on a paper headband (use popsicle sticks behind each feather to make them stand up), tom-tom from a coffee can, and a tomahawk from construction paper and a stick.

TV reporter—Microphone (made from paper towel tube with rolled up socks stuffed in one end), camera (made from a box with toilet paper roll taped on for a lens), a tie or scarf, and a cereal box for a commercial.

Goodie box. Buy a small plastic carrying case and make it the home for all of the miscellaneous little pieces of junk that children accumulate through the years—birthday party favors, prizes from Cracker Jack and cereal boxes, a favorite penny, a Christmas card that Grandma sent them. You'll always know where their treasures are and it will entertain your children from time to time to "clean it out."

YOUR CHILD'S LIBRARY

Your children are ready for picture books that tell stories, books that teach about concepts like time, shapes, numbers, and nature, and fairy tale books. There won't be enough hours in the day to read all of the wonderful books that are available. You'll no doubt need to visit the library more often now, since you won't be able to purchase everything you'll want to read. Here is just a sampling of the best. Christian books are marked with an asterisk.

BENNETT CERF'S BOOK OF RIDDLES (Random House, 1960)—Preschoolers usually love riddles, and this book contains some of the best.

ANNO'S COUNTING HOUSE (Mitsumasa Anno, Philomel Books, 1982)—This is the most sophisticated of the counting books. Two full pages of instructions are given. Through playing the games, your child will be introduced to all sorts of advanced mathematical concepts. But most of all, she'll have a wonderful time seeing ten little people move from room to room in *Anno's Counting House*.

WHO'S A FRIEND OF THE WATER SPURTING WHALE? * (Sanna Anderson Baker, Illustrated by Tomie dePaola, David C. Cook 1987)—The poetry and art celebrate the biblical concept of God's care for His creatures.

THE LION BOOK OF CHILDREN'S PRAYERS * (Mary Editor Batchelor, Lion, 1977)—A comprehensive collection of over 200 children's prayers. This volume could be used as a book of poetry, as a family devotional, or simply as a read aloud.

STONE SOUP (Marcia Brown, Charles Scribner, 1975)—Marcia Brown specializes in the interpretation of fairy tales and has won several Caldecott awards for her work. How do three hungry soldiers trick an entire village into donating vegetables and beef to make soup from a stone? Read this one aloud to find out. Other favorite fairy tales include: *Once a Mouse*, *Cindrella*, *Puss in Boots*, *Dick Whittington and His Cat*, and *The Steadfast Tin Soldier*.

MIKE MULLIGAN AND HIS STEAM SHOVEL (Virginia Lee Burton, Houghton Mifflin 1939)—You can still pick this one up in paperback. Children never tire of the story.

MY VERY FIRST BOOK OF WORDS (Eric Carle, Thomas Y. Crowell, 1974)—Your children can have fun learning ten new words as they match the word on the top of the page with pictures on the bottom. Illustrations are simple and colorful Carle classics. There are several others in the series including *My Very First Book of Shapes*. Also read the other classic Carle stories like *The Very Hungry Caterpillar*, *The Mixed-Up Chameleon*, and *The Secret Birthday Message*.

ED EMBERLEY'S ABC (Ed Emberley, Little, Brown, 1978)—Ed Emberley's distinctive style will tickle your funny bone while it helps your preschooler learn to write the letters of the alphabet. For each letter there is an animal doing something that results in another letter being formed.

THE GINGERBREAD MAN (Paul Galdone, Clarion Books, 1975)—Galdone does a masterful job of interpreting the best folk and fairy tales. His illustrations have a whimsy that brings new life to the stories. Sample them all! *The Little Red Hen*, *The Three Bears*, *The Three Billy Goats Gruff*, *The Magic Porridge Pot*, *Henny Penny*, *Little Tuppen*, and *Old Mother Hubbard and Her Dog* are among the many titles.

LITTLE TOOT (Hardi Gramatky, G.P. Putnam, 1939)—The well-told tale of a little tugboat who has a hard time living up to the expectations of Father and Grandfather Toot. Also read *Hercules, Loopy, Sparky, Little Toot on the Thames,* and *Little Toot on the Grand Canal.*

*THE BOY WHO GAVE HIS LUNCH AWAY** (Dave Hill, Illustrated by Betty Wind, Concordia, Arch Books 1967)—Arch paperback Bible stories in rhyme have withstood the test of time. Children adore them! There are now over a hundred in the series by different authors and illustrators.

DIG, DRILL, DUMP, FILL (Tana Hoban, Greenwillow, 1975)—Full page black-and-white photographs of machines of many kinds will fascinate your inquisitive preschooler. Hoban's other books—*Shapes and Things; Circles, Triangles, and Squares; Over, Under, and Through; Round and Round and Round;* and *Push-Pull, Empty-Full* are also ideal for teaching concepts. If you enjoy photography yourself, you will appreciate Hoban's work.

BREAD AND JAM FOR FRANCES (Russell Hoban, Illustrated by Lillian Hoban, Harper & Row, 1964)—Frances is by far the most enchanting of all animal characters in children's literature. This badger will win your heart as she refuses to eat anything but bread and jam. Also read: *A Baby Sister for Frances, Bedtime for Frances, Best Friends for Frances,* and *A Birthday for Frances.*

DON'T FORGET THE BACON (Pat Hutchins, Greenwillow, 1976)—Although the text is simple, don't be fooled. The humor is much more sophisticated. Read these titles also: *The Wind Blew, Clocks and More Clocks, The Surprise Party,* and *Titch.*

THUMBELINA (Susan Jeffers, Dial Press, 1979)—Susan Jeffers is a multi-talented artist whose interpretations of fairy tales and poetry are remarkable. Her illustrations add another element of appreciation to the familiar fairy tales. Look for these other titles: *Three Jovial Huntsmen*, *Close Your Eyes*, and *Hansel and Gretel.*

Ezra Jack Keats/Steven Kellogg/Robert Kraus
Read anything by these three gentlemen. Their books are appealing to children, have wonderful humor and illustrations, and will keep you and your children entertained for hours.

TIME (Jan Pienkowski, Julian Messner, 1980)—If your preschooler is fascinated with clocks, pick up this small book that contains clocks showing different times and events throughout the day and night.

COLORS (John J. Reiss, Bradbury Press, 1971)—This is the best of the color books. You'll have a wonderful time looking at all of the "things to eat, things to wear, and things to pat" in vivid colors.

CURIOUS GEORGE (H.A. Rey, Houghton Mifflin, 1941)—Curious George probably entertained you when you were a child. There is something endearing about this curious monkey most likely associated with his ingenious ability to outwit almost every human he meets.

LEIF LIKES TO PLAY* (Christine Harder Tangvald, David C. Cook, 1986)—Leif is an irrepressible waif ("My Friend Leif" Series) who encounters the unlikely wherever he goes. He'll tickle your funny bone, while reminding you and your child to give thanks to God for the gifts of laughter and imagination. (Other titles are *Leif Needs a Bath*, *Leif Likes to Count*, and *Leif Cleans His Room.*)

IRA SLEEPS OVER (Bernard Waber, Houghton, 1972)—Ira can hardly wait to sleep over at his best friend's house.

Naturally he plans to take along his teddy bear, until his sister ridicules his plan. When he discovers that his friend Reggie's bear is called "Foo Foo," Ira returns home to get his own beloved "Tah Tah." Other titles by Waber that make good read-alouds are *Lyle, Lyle, Crocodile*; *Lyle and the Birthday Party*; and *The House on East 88th Street*.

ARTS AND CRAFTS SUPPLIES

See the materials listed under "Toys You Already Have" for a beginning list of items to collect. Here are some others.

Junk. Save beads, old jewlery, rickrack, feathers, toothpicks, corks, nails, pipe cleaners, bobby pins, macaroni, seeds, beans, spools, stars, stickers, cotton balls, empty film cannisters, old string, broken shoelaces, and old greeting cards.

Finger paint. Use the recipe from Chapter 7 or graduate to purchased finger paints to try something different. Be sure to use shiny paper for best results.

Paints and brushes. In addition to the brushes of different sizes and shapes you've collected along the way, add some of the very inexpensive "foam" brushes that are available at the paint or hardware store.

Chalk, markers, crayons, pens, and colored pencils. Buy non-toxic, washable materials whenever possible. Otherwise, provide close supervision. (The washable markers even washed out of my silk lamp shades when Emily decorated them during her nap time.)

Yarns, fabrics. Make friends with a seamstress who can give you remnants if you don't sew yourself. Preschoolers love to work with different kinds of fabric.

Papers. See the list in the Paper Box under "Toys You Already Have."

Containers of every sort. Save Styrofoam trays, yogurt containers, coffee cans, cardboard boxes of all sizes, heavy plastic drawstring shopping bags, heavy paper shopping bags, aluminum tins from pot pies or tarts, and plastic margarine tubs.

Food. It's amazing the number of food items that make wonderful craft and collage materials: rice, beans, pasta of all shapes and sizes, seeds, and cereal.

Play dough, baking dough, and commercial clay. Although there are many variations on the play dough recipe, the best mixture I've found is the one in Chapter 7. My friend Terri and her preschooler, Michael, recently ran a comparison test for me on all the popular recipes and pronounced that one "Great!" Once you've tried homemade, buy some commercial clay or Play Doh at the store for a different creative experience.

Art equipment. Buy scissors, Elmer's Glue, paste, rubber cement, stapler, paper punch, ruler, protractor, unlined index cards, and rubber stamp pads of various colors. See if your stationery store has unsold or defective rubber stamps you can have. Pick up an old typewriter at a garage sale.

Sources for pictures. Collect old textbooks, encyclopedias, magazines, and catalogs to cut up. Garage sales are good places to find old printed materials for cutting and pasting. Some school districts give away old textbooks from time to time.

PARENT RESOURCE LIBRARY
Consult the resources in Chapters 6 and 7. These books will continue to be of help.

LANGUAGE AND CONCEPT DEVELOPMENT
As your children move into the final phase of development before entering school, you will notice that many of the activities are specifically designed for school readiness. Once again, I'll offer some words of wisdom.

Don't pressure your children. Don't expect mastery of a skill or task the first or second or third time you try it. And above all, don't get hung up on teaching your children to read. Just read aloud, talk with them, and participate in a low-key way in the games and activities that you'll find in this section. Let nature takes its course!

If you've been following the recommendations from Chapters 6 and 7, then your children already have an excellent language foundation. Keep up what you've been doing and add the following.

Talking. Continue to label, label, label. Give your children as much vocabulary as you can. They will probably remember the big words most easily. (Have you ever met a preschooler who didn't know all of the names of dinosaurs that most adults can barely pronouce?)

Use a variety of words to describe things; don't just use "good" and "nice." Take each new experience you have as an opportunity to learn new words. When you visit Midas to get a new muffler, talk about mufflers, tail pipes, exhaust systems, and welding. When you visit the greenhouse to choose new plants for the garden, talk about marigolds, impatiens, zinnias, and geraniums. When you make a new recipe, talk about woks, peanut oil, soy sauce, bean sprouts, water chestnuts, and pea pods.

Conversation. Your toddler can now engage in fairly complex conversations with you. Expand on her talents by asking questions like "What do you like about ice cream?" "What do you dislike about pizza?" (if she does indeed dislike it). Encourage her to be specific. Is it the taste, the texture, or the color? Ask her to tell you a story. If that's too difficult, you start the story and ask her to finish it. Practice telephone conversations using the play telephone. Pop a few finger puppets into your purse (our favorites were the Sesame Street characters Bert and Ernie) and have conversations with finger puppets the next time you have to wait somewhere. Talk about what you will do tomorrow and then have your toddler retell the day's plan in correct sequence. Ask her to tell you how to make a sandwich or pudding. (Choose things that you have made before.)

Concept words. Before your children get to kindergarten they should know dozens of different concepts. The best way to learn them is through constant usage and seeing concrete examples. Try to make them a part of daily conversation in the next couple of years.

Size words: big, bigger, biggest, small, smaller, smallest, short, shorter, shortest, tall, taller, tallest, long, longer, longest, thin, thinner, thinnest, fat, fatter, fattest.

Shape words: circle, ball, cylinder, round, square, cube, rectangle, triangle, pyramid, cone.

Position words: on top of, on the bottom of, under, behind, in the middle, next to, in front of, left, right, on, in, inside, outside.

Show and tell. Whenever you go somewhere, collect something to bring back. Have a show and tell time when the family is together. Let your preschooler "have the floor" to tell about her treasure. These need not be expensive or elaborate. Bring back a shiny stone from the park, the register tape from the grocery store, or two straws from McDonald's. The important part is sharing information and experiences.

Why and what games. Give your toddler a little of her own medicine—you pose the questions. Why do we make our bed after we get up? What would happen if we put our ice cubes in the sunshine? What else could this (show her any common household object) be used for? What happens after we go to bed? What happens after we put our cookies in the oven? Answering these kinds of questions helps develop higher level thinking skills. Just don't treat them like an examination. If your child doesn't know the answer, give her a hint . . . and try an easier question the next time.

Memory games. Next time you come home from the grocery store, ask your preschooler to help you put the items away. Select five different items that she can put away. When she is finished, ask her to recall what the items were.

For another easy memory game, place several different objects on a table (e.g., a bobby pin, a paper clip, a pencil, a whistle, and a comb). Name two of the objects and ask her to pick them up in that order. When she can pick up two, add one or two more. Change the objects and try it again.

See if your preschooler can follow a series of directions, such as, "Clap your hands and then touch your knees." "Blink your eyes and then wiggle your fingers." "Kiss your hand, clap your hands three times, and then stick out your tongue." Don't be discouraged if she can't remember several at one time. This takes practice.

Riddles and word games. Riddles are wonderful ways to explore language and develop problem solving and thinking skills. They are also just plain fun. *Bennett Cerf's Book of Animal Riddles* (Random House, 1964) is one example to get you started. The library has many more. It doesn't matter if both of you already have heard the riddle a dozen times. Your toddler will delight in many retellings.

Poetry. Read poetry often as a way to introduce rhyme and rhythm into your children's lives. Being able to hear that different letters make different sounds is crucial to success in reading. Give your children lots of opportunities.

READING AND READING READINESS

Reading Aloud. Of course you're continuing to read aloud every day. By now, your child should be attentive for longer periods of time, with many favorite books she wants to hear read aloud, and from time to time pretending to read on her own. Don't stop now. The critical years are ahead.

Your child is beginning to associate the written and spoken word and is soaking up information, vocabulary, and concepts every time you read aloud to her. Take books with you wherever you go—shoe store, dentist, doctor, barber shop, laundromat. It's amazing how much time we spend waiting. Your preschooler should not waste a minute of that time.

Book talk. Now that your child has a longer attention span and the stories you're reading have characters and plots, you can take some time for talking about the books you read. Once again, keep it low key and respond to your child's needs. If she doesn't appear interested in lengthy discussions, then don't force them. But if you can, talk about the title and the cover. Try to connect some of the characters in the book with your child's experiences. ("Remember, you liked bread and jam for supper just like Frances did.") Point out new words or concepts to your child and ask if she has any questions. During your reading, stop occasionally and talk about words or pictures on the page. Before you turn a page, ask your child to predict what will happen next.

Even more book talk. If you sense your child is ready for higher level discussions about the books you are reading, relate characters in the books to real life characters. ("Mommy gets mixed up in the kitchen just like Amelia Bedelia.") Draw parallells between events in stories that are similar or different to your child's life. ("You know, you remind me of Ira in *Ira Sleeps Over*. Do you know why?")

Magazines. Check out several popular children's magazines from the library and ask your child to help you choose one that you will subscribe to for her. Don't check anything out that you wouldn't feel comfortable buying. If you need help, consult the children's librarian.

Lotto games. Lotto games are wonderful for letting children figure out relationships between objects. You can start by matching identical pictures (two cats in exactly the same pose), move on to matching pictures that are similar but not the same (a cat and a kitten), try objects that are just related (a cow and a glass of milk), and then try some real puzzlers.

Mr. Rogers relates a wonderful story in his playbook about a friend who developed a challenging lotto game that took his daughter several weeks to complete. Each pair of pictures was related but took some higher level thinking to figure out. One example was a picture of her father and a picture of a balloon popping (pop was the critical concept there). If you're very creative try your hand at creating your own lotto.

Writing. Let your child use a typewriter to create her own stories. Staple the pages together and let her make illustrations. No matter that you cannot read what she has written. You have missed the point if you think otherwise. Or write down a story as she dictates it and then let her do the illustrations.

Scrapbooks. Make scrapbooks by cutting pictures out of magazines and pasting them on paper to make a clothing book, a baby book, an animal book, or a people book. Make a scrapbook of places you've visited. The possibilities are endless.

Alphabet. All parents are eager to teach their child the alphabet. It seems to be the first indication of reading readiness. Learning the alphabet song is fun but doesn't indicate any real understanding of the letters.

If you're serious about teaching your child the alphabet, here's the best way. Work on one letter at a time. Spend at least a week or two on the letter. Practice writing each new letter in sand or fingerpaint. Form the letters in play dough, cookie dough, or pretzel dough. Cut the letter out of sandpaper and glue it on cardboard. Trace over it. Make a large letter out of paste on construction paper and have your child stick cereal, beans, dried noodles, or buttons on the wet paste. Look for each new letter on cereal boxes, signs, newspapers, and books. Circle the letter on the pages of magazines or newspapers. Start with capital letters and then move to lower case. Make a matching game with pairs of cards made of the capital and lower-case letters. Start an alphabet book allowing a page for each letter. Count how many times you see your letter during the day or during a car trip.

Message board. Write messages on the refrigerator with magnetic letters: "Hello, Emily," "I Love You, Patrick," or "Please don't eat the ice cream." Soon your preschooler will be writing his own messages: "Stop, Mom," or "Hello, Dad."

Sticky notes. Post-it notes are wonderful for leaving messages. Stick them up on your child's dresser or closet door and see if she can figure out what they say. If not, she'll come running for a translation.

Magnetic letter match-up. Make flash cards for each of the upper-case letters using magic marker. Spread the cards on the floor and let your preschooler match each with the corresponding magnetic letter. If she is too overwhelmed with twenty-six, just use the letters that spell her first name. Then move to her last name.

The letter game. Think of items from the store that begin with the same letter: I went to the store and I bought beans, bacon, and butter. I went to the store and I bought cocoa, cabbage, and carrots. I went to the store and bought pizza, pasta, and pie. Use only words that begin with consonants, since they are much easier for preschoolers to hear.

Sight words on the street. Sight words are those that children read quickly because they have memorized them. Make flash cards for the sight words your children see on "Sesame Street" and out in the community and then find them as you are out and about. Examples are: bus stop, telephone, stop, don't walk, exit, one way, wet paint, yield, danger, school, mail, open, closed, cold, hot, street, walk, no parking, in, out, handicapped, men, women. If they can read the flash cards, you will know they are really reading and not just recognizing the word from visual clues and symbols.

Labeling. If you want to teach your child more sight words, label things around the house. Put 3 x 5 cards on household appliances, furniture, and whatever else you care to label.

VALUES

Manners. In addition to modeling the kinds of manners you want your children to have, you can begin to explain how good manners make others feel. Children will forget to say please and thank you on occasion, but publicly embarrassing them or forcing the issue too often can backfire. A better strategy is to discuss a social situation ahead of time so children can be prepared when a response is called for.

Following rules. Continue to keep your rules simple and short. Be sensitive to your child's need for rest and nutrition and don't expect too much from her when she is tired or hungry. Perfectly wonderful children can often turn into monsters without proper rest or food.

Sharing. Give your child opportunities to play with others and begin to share and work cooperatively. Don't expect too much in the beginning. The concept of giving up beloved playthings is a difficult one for preschoolers to understand. If you're expecting company, talk ahead of time about which toys your child would be willing to share. If there's a special toy, put it away to head off possible conflict and embarrassment.

Self-esteem. Basic to love and acceptance of others is a healthy level of self-esteem. There are many specific things you as a parent can do to nuture self-esteem in your children:

- Praise your children for their accomplishments and achievements.

- Accept your children for what they are. A child's feelings of personal worth will never be greater than the worth her family finds in her.
- Cultivate the lively art of communication in your household. Connect with your children on a personal level.
- Model a strong feeling of self-worth, independence, and responsibility. Begin now to believe in yourself and your worth as a parent.
- Foster the unique and special talents and qualities that you find in your children.
- Show love and physical affection often. Children need to feel their parents' touch of love and encouragement.

Caring and sharing projects. Adopt a neighbor or older adult as a special friend. Help your child find the delight in making and doing things for others. Do something special for someone in need. Translate the words of the Gospels into actions that your children can see. If your child receives a gift, help her write a simple thank you note. Her contribution can be to draw a picture while you write the words.

Stories and prayers to teach values. Continue to use read-alouds to teach the Christian values you want to impart to your children. Read a Bible story every day. Pray before bedtime. Choose stories that appeal to your children and say prayers that are simple and meaningful to them.

PHYSICAL DEVELOPMENT AND PLAY ACTIVITIES

The most important contribution that you can make to your children's development during this period is to structure play without getting involved. Provide the materials and the environment, but don't get in there and try to "run the show." Preschoolers need opportunities to develop independence and make judgments. They do this through play, both independent and group.

These suggestions for activities can be done by children themselves. If you provide a basic idea and the equipment, they will do the rest! Don't be disappointed if they change or throw out your idea and do something different. That's the beginning of learning to make choices and decisions.

Dress-up clothes. In addition to the Pretend Boxes mentioned previously, keep a box of discarded grownups' clothes. An old suit with a vest, ties, junk jewelery, aprons, hats, and shoes are the basis for wonderful imaginative play. If you have an old trunk to store the clothes in, so much the better. If you really enjoy dressing up, you can also consult *Easy to Make Costumes* by Frieda Gates (Harvey House, 1978).

Pretend play. Take a pretend trip. A shopping bag or box can be your suitcase. Pack up some old clothes. Line up the chairs for a plane, bus, or train. Take off for a warmer climate.

Basketball. Give your child a three-inch diameter ball or beanbag and have her try to throw it into a large wastebasket or box. Start close up and move farther away as she becomes more successful.

Basic motor skills. Help develop body coordination by encouraging your children to practice such skills as catching, throwing, kicking a ball, jumping a rope, hanging, swinging, hopping on one or two feet, galloping, climbing, skipping, doing jumping jacks, and walking along a balance beam. Remember, you're having fun! We are not looking for Olympic gold medalists! Visit some different parks and school playgrounds to use various types of equipment.

Daily exercises. If you have a daily workout, either running or aerobics, encourage your child to join in. You can also add these daily exercises to your child's routine: (1) Try to balance on one foot. At first your child will need to hop to keep upright, but later encourage her to stand still. (2) Hold your fingers out to your child as though to pick her up. Let her grab your fingers or your thumbs and jump up as you lift her to your chest. If her grip weakens, your free fingers can grasp her wrists to help out. This strengthens your child's arm and hand muscles. (3) With your child facing away from you, hold her with the same hand grip, then have her lift her legs straight up in front, open, close, and lower them again. This is good for posture and abdominal muscles.

Jumping game. Ask your child to jump up and down twice. Jump over an object forward, backward, sideways, or any series. Hop twice, hop on one foot, hop backward, hop twice and then jump. These games are good for memory as well as motor development.

Out-of-doors play. Preschoolers should spend time out of doors every day, except in the most inclement or severe weather. Get preschoolers used to playing on their own. Keep a watchful eye on their activities, but don't interfere or oversee. They can be loud, messy, active, and out of control—without bothering anyone. Make sure you have plenty of balls, jump ropes, trucks, riding toys (Big Wheels, trikes, kiddie cars, tractors or scooters are all suitable), wagons, and outdoor equipment.

Depending on the weather, outdoor play will involve sand, water, or dirt. Visit a park or playground, take a ride, or walk around the block. In the summer, set up a wading pool or sprinkler. In winter, get out the sleds and saucers. Older preschoolers can sometimes handle simple roller skates or double runner ice skates. My theory was "keep them moving and they'll sleep better at night."

MUSIC

The suggestions that were made in Chapters 6 and 7 for younger children are also appropriate for preschoolers. Expand your repertoire of music each year.

Movement to music. Help your children respond creatively to a variety of music. Clap, march, tiptoe, gallop like a horse, fly like a bird, hop like a bunny, sway like a flower in the wind, walk slowly. Move the arms in a circular motion, swing them stiffly, or let them hang limp. Raise, lower, and bend the body.

Singing games. Add movements and motions to favorite songs to create games. Favorites are "The Farmer in the Dell," "Ring Around the Rosey," "Here We Go Round the Mulberry Bush," "Here We Go Looby Loo," and "London Bridge Is Falling Down." Invite some of your child's friends over to play these games. The more the merrier.

Musical instruments. If you haven't yet helped your child make instruments, then try your hand at making some now. These ideas are so simple, preschoolers can do them on their own. Two pot lids make a cymbal. Put some dry macaroni in a flour shaker. (Make sure the top is on securely.) Wooden spoons become drumsticks for an oatmeal box. Cover a comb with wax paper and hum away. Take an empty shoe box and stretch ten different rubber bands around it to make a guitar. Tape some sandpaper on blocks for a different musical sound. Cardboard tubes of varying sizes make wonderful horns.

COOKING AND HOUSEHOLD FUN

This is an arena in which preschoolers can really blossom, and you can begin to teach many useful lifetime skills. Preschoolers are quite capable helpers and delight in doing "grown up" things.

Cooking for the under threes. Some kitchen tasks may be too challenging, but creating instant pudding, tearing up lettuce for salads, mixing up Jiffy Mix muffins or brownies, or baking cookies from Pillsbury Cookie Rolls are sure winners.

Kitchen vocabulary. The kitchen is a perfect place to work on language development. Children can learn the following new words: boil, chop, grind, tear, mash, stir, mix, sift, shake, measure, slice, bake, and fry. Introduce them to such fascinating kitchen implements as the melon ball scooper, wire whip, nested measuring cups, egg beater, hard boiled egg slicer, and apple corer.

Household jobs for preschoolers. Don't take the attitude that "I can do it faster myself." Your preschoolers will miss out on dozens of learning opportunities. They probably won't finish the job the first time, but keep providing opportunities.

- Sponge up a spill.
- Clean the silver.
- Wash windows or mirrors.
- Wipe dishes (only the plastic ones, please).
- Put things away.
- Sort laundry.

- Dust.
- Fold clothes (small flat items are best).
- Vacuum.
- Clean fingerprints.
- Wash doll clothes and/or play dishes.
- Scrub bathtub (be sure to use a mild soap).
- Sort the mail.
- Help make the shopping list.
- Put dirty clothes in hamper.
- Pick up old newspapers.
- Sort the silverware.
- Set the table (silverware or plastic dishes).
- Wash woodwork, refrigerator, stove, chairs, counter.
- Wash vegetables.

Practical life skills. While you're worrying about reading, math, and science, don't forget to systematically teach your children these practical life skills: opening and closing drawers, pouring, dusting, carrying a chair, folding a napkin, setting a table, washing dishes, washing hands, washing a table, sweeping the floor, polishing silver, shining shoes, lacing a shoe, replacing tops of bottles (four to six bottles and jars of varying sizes with tops will help), using a dropper, and cutting with blunt-end scissors.

Cooking for threes, fours, and fives. If you'd like some help in getting started with cooking, sample the following excellent books:

- *Pickle in the Middle and Other Easy Snacks* (Frances Zweifel, Harper & Row, 1979) contains simple recipes that preschoolers can make. The book is fun to read aloud even if you don't make the recipes.
- *Let's Make Soup* (Hanna Lyons Johnson, Lothrop, Lee, and Shepard Company, 1976) will take you through the soup making process step by step.
- *The All-Around Pumpkin Book* (Margery Cuyler, Holt, Rinehart, and Winston, 1980) will tell you everything you ever wanted to know about cooking or crafting with pumpkins.

Sure-fire favorites: pretzels, cookies, and butter. Making pretzels gives you and your preschooler a chance to mix, knead, and punch. The dough is easy to work with. Your child can help. The most fun is baking shapes and letters that your child can recognize.

HOMEMADE PRETZELS
Ingredients for Step One:

1 package. of yeast   3/4 cup warm water
4 cups flour   1/2 teaspoon sugar
1/2 teaspoon salt

Ingredients for Step Two:

1/2 egg, beaten   Kosher salt (optional)

Step One: Add yeast to water, stirring until dissolved. Add salt and sugar; stir. Add flour; stir. Knead lightly on floured surface until completely smooth. Store in greased container with plastic wrap on top for at least one hour, or overnight. Punch dough down. Divide into sixteen equal portions. Roll the portions into a "snake" with your hands. Shape into pretzels (or whatever letter or shape you want) and place on an aluminum-foil-lined cookie sheet.

Step Two: Brush with egg, sprinkle lightly with salt, and bake at 425 degrees for 15 minutes.

BUTTER COOKIES

1 cup butter (2 Sticks)
1 1/2 cups sifted confectioners sugar
1 egg   1 teaspoon vanilla
2 1/2 cups sifted flour   1 teaspoon baking soda
1 teaspoon cream of tartar   1/4 teaspoon salt

Cream butter. Add sugar gradually; cream until fluffy. Add unbeaten egg and vanilla. Beat well. Sift together dry ingredients. Blend into creamed mixture. Divide dough. Prepare cookies in variations you prefer (see below). Place on an ungreased cookie sheet and bake at 400 degrees.

I've made this cookie recipe for twenty-five years. When my children started helping me, they were always intrigued by how many different kinds of cookies we could make from the same dough. Here are some suggestions:

Butter Crispies (rolled). Chill dough. Roll on well-floured pastry cloth to 1/8″ thick. Cut with floured cookie cutters. Bake about 6 minutes. When done, these can be frosted with butter cream frosting or sprinkled with any kind of decoration.

Snowballs. To half of the cookie dough add 3/4 cup ground walnuts. Chill. Roll dough into balls the size of marbles. Bake 8 to 10 minutes. Roll at once in confectioners sugar. Cool. Roll again in sugar. Makes about 2 1/2 dozen.

Butter Fingers. To half of the cookie dough add 1/2 cup chopped nuts and 1/4 cup chopped candied cherries. Chill. Shape into oblongs the size of a little finger. Bake 8 to 10 minutes. Sprinkle while hot with granulated sugar.

Trixie Treats. Chill half the dough and mold it into balls the size of walnuts. Roll in mixture of 2 tablespoons sugar and 1 teaspoon cinnamon. Bake 8 to 10 minutes. Makes about 2 dozen.

Butter Thinsies (Refrigerator Cookie). Form dough into rolls (2 inches thick). Wrap in wax paper. Chill until firm. Slice 1/8″ thick. Sprinkle with finely chopped nuts or coconut. Bake 6 minutes.

Chocolate Mint Creams. To half of the dough add 1 square of unsweetened chocolate, melted and cooled. Form dough into rolls (2 inches thick). Chill. Slice 1/8″ thick. Bake 8 minutes. Cool. Put two cookies together with Mint Cream Filling (Butter Cream Frosting with peppermint flavoring and a hint of green food coloring).

Jewel Cluster. Drop dough by half teaspoon on cookie sheet. Press candied fruit into each. Bake 8 minutes.

Molasses Spice-eez. To half of the dough add 2 tablespoons molasses, 1/2 teaspoon ginger, 1 teaspoon cinnamon, and 1/4 teaspoon nutmeg. Chill at least 1/2 hour. Roll 1/8″ thick on well-floured surface. Cut into patterns with cookie cutters.

HOMEMADE BUTTER
1/2 pint heavy whipping cream
1 pint jar with tight fitting lid

Put the whipping cream into the jar, making sure the lid is screwed on tightly and the jar is held firmly in the hands of the child who shakes it and shakes it and shakes it some more. Butter and buttermilk will be the end products.

(My friend Terri and her son Michael used the mixer for five minutes and then shook for five to ten minutes. They put in a popsicle stick when shaking for the butter to form on. My kindergarten teacher puts a marble in the jar; this also speeds up the process.)

Gingerbread House. If you're feeling especially ambitious, check out *It's a Gingerbread House: Bake It! Build It! Eat It!* by Vera B. Williams (Greenwillow Books, 1978). This marvelous little book tells you how to make a gingerbread house in easy to follow steps. My children and I made it and the directions actually work. (This is not always the case in books of this type). The house lasted for several holiday seasons wrapped tightly in plastic.

ARTS, CRAFTS, AND CREATIVITY

A few words of warning are in order before you attempt art projects with preschoolers. Don't ever argue with your child about what something is. He knows. You don't! Let your child cut and paste what and where he wants (not on furniture or walls, of course). Let him make mistakes and solve problems on his own. You provide the materials and simple directions. If he chooses not to follow them, that's fine. He needs to be pleased with the end product, not you.

Books to help you. If you like to sample lots of ideas, try *How to Make Snop Snappers and Other Fine Things* by Robert Lopshire (Greenwillow Books, 1977). It contains wonderful simple little toys that are made out of Styrofoam cups, glue, and other such junk. We checked this book out of the library dozens of times.

Ed Emberley has imaginative drawing ideas for the budding artist. *Ed Emberley's Book of Faces* (Little, Brown,

1975), *Ed Emberley's Great Thumbprint Drawing Book* (Little, Brown, 1977), and *Ed Emberley's Picture Pie: A Circle Drawing Book* (Little, Brown, 1984) are a few.

Painting. Finger painting (with our homemade paint) and easel painting with tempera are still very popular activities. Don't forget a dropcloth for the floor and a paint shirt for the child. Make sure your child helps with the clean-up. Cleaning up is always part of any activity.

Printmaking. You can use tempera paints and do printing with sponges, fruits, and vegetables.

Construction. Continue to collect junk to make sculptures and collages.

Box construction. Shoe box vehicles, milk carton boats, egg carton toys, box towns, doll houses, simple dioramas, and musical instruments are all examples of things your child can make with a discarded box. Ask friends to save good boxes for use in play and then let your child's imagination do the rest.

Drawing with markers, crayons, and colored pencils. Let your preschooler scribble and draw to her heart's content. Some weeks you'll wish you owned stock in a paper company. But just remember that your child's imagination and creativity will only be fully developed if she has a chance to create without regard for public opinion (and yours).

Sprinkle art. Squeeze a small bottle of white glue over a piece of paper. You can make a free form design, make letters, or even a simple picture. Sprinkle the wet design with glitter, cornmeal, sugar, salt, rice, confetti, seeds, pine needles, or sand. Shake off the excess into the garbage or a storage container if you want to reuse the material. Let the painting dry.

Styrofoam art. Use a block of Styrofoam packing material. Find a variety of things to stick in it and make a free form sculpture. Materials could include: pipe cleaners, wire, dowels, broom straws, old jewelry, chains, beads, feathers, toothpicks, skewers, corks, straws, nails, screws, yarn, macaroni, flowers, or craft sticks. Use clean Styrofoam trays from the grocery store to make a weaving. Make cuts at the top and bottom edges of the tray. String yarn back and forth through the cuts. Weave fabrics, feathers, ribbon, or other colors and types of yarn through the strings. Tape ends of weaving to back of tray.

Lunch bag puppets. The way in which the bottom of a lunch bag folds over looks just like a face and mouth that is moving. If you make two holes in the bag's bottom you can put two fingers through them and give your puppet ears. Decorate with crayons and "junk."

Attachment puzzle. The book *Learn at Home the Sesame Street Way* (Simon and Schuster, 1979) suggests the following wonderful activity: Set up an empty egg carton with these items in each of the compartments: two paper clips, a threaded needle, two scraps of cloth, a toothpick, a cork or small Styrofoam scrap, a piece of wire or pipe cleaner, a button, a section of plastic straw, two rubber bands, wood or cardboard scrap with a nail hole punched in it, two scraps of paper, and a six-inch length of string. Ask your child to connect as many different items as she can. The beauty of this activity is its open-endedness. There is no right answer. Your child can test her creative problem solving ability.

MATH AND SCIENCE

Even if the words mathematics and science strike terror in your heart, don't be dismayed. Kids are just naturally interested in these subjects, and there are lots of books to help. A fascinating book that makes complicated science concepts seem simple is *Rainbows, Curve Balls and Other Wonders of the Natural World Explained* by Ira Flatow (Harper & Row, 1989).

I've suggested other books in the sections that follow, but don't overlook the non-fiction section of your public library for dozens more that will help your preschooler become more aware of science and math concepts.

Nature walks. Be sure to take time to observe all of God's wonders in nature. Clouds moving, leaves blowing, branches swaying, the moon and stars, insects flying and crawling, the parts of a flower, acorns, squirrels, and birds feeding in your backyard.

Growing crystals. Break up some charcoal briquets in an old piepan. Add two Tablespoons each of salt, water, ammonia, and bluing. As the liquid evaporates, crystals will grow.

Growing plants. If you didn't try the planting experiences in Chapter 7, see if you're ready now. If you need help, consult *How to Grow a Jelly Glass Farm* by Kathy Mandry and Joe Toto (Pantheon Books, 1974). Your child will also enjoy reading *Your First Garden Book* by Marc Brown (Little, Brown, 1981). If you want a comprehensive gardening guide, buy *The Victory Garden Kids' Book: A Beginner's Guide to Growing Vegetables, Fruits, and Flowers* by Marjorie Waters (Houghton, Mifflin Co., 1988).

Growth book. Plant a fast-growing tree or shrub and measure it every week. Keep records of its growth rate. You can do the same with fast growing flowers.

Weather and temperature charts. Perhaps you've already charted the daily weather on a calendar. Mount a thermometer in the garage or patio where your child can see it and chart the daily temperatures.

"Hairy" Sponge. You can grow "hair" on a sponge. Wet a bath sponge, sprinkle it with grass seed, put it on an old plate, cover it with a clear glass dish, and place it in a sunny location. Remove the glass dish when you see sprouts appear.

Bright and shiny copper pennies. You'll need newspapers, 4 tablespoons of salt, 1/2 cup vinegar, 1 cup water, an old glass bottle, lots of "dirty" pennies, and an old kitchen spoon. Combine the salt, vinegar, and water. Stir until all of the salt is dissolved. Now add the pennies and continue to stir. When the pennies are clean, dip them out with the spoon and place them to dry on some paper towels.

Science in action. Use everyday happenings to point out scientific principles at work. Letting go of a balloon filled with air shows jet propulsion. Drinking straws help explain suction, a vacuum, and pressure. Brushing your hair or touching a metal switch after scuffing over the carpet illustrates static electricity. The variation in amounts of daylight helps explain the change of seasons. A cake mixer is a good object lesson in centrifugal force. A bathtub filled with water can help you define immersion and displacement (when the water rises in the tub after you have gotten in).

Collections. Collect leaves, shells, insects, or rocks. Check out books from the library that help you identify your specimens.

Fun with eggs. Try some simple experiments with eggs found in *Egg-Ventures: First Science Experiments* by Harry Milgrom (E.P. Dutton, 1974).

Body T-shirt. Paint the internal organs (heart, lungs, stomach, etc.) on the front of a T-shirt. Label the names.

Magnifying glass. Get an inexpensive magnifying glass and look at your hands, a leaf, an earthworm, a spider web, a drop of water, a fly, a flower, a snowflake, bark, plants, moss, grass, ants, and hair.

Scientific tools. In addition to the magnifying glass, you can give your child screwdrivers and hammers to take apart old appliances, a thermometer, a flashlight, a pocket mirror, magnets, and an inexpensive microscope (save the good one until she's older). An inexpensive camera also makes a wonderful tool to sharpen your child's observation of the world around him.

Bubble blowing. Mix up a batch of bubbles, find some straws, funnels, or a twisted coat hanger, and prepare for fascinating fun.

BUBBLE BLOWING MIX
1 cup dishwashing detergent (Joy or Dawn works best)
2 cups warm water
3 tablespoons glycerine (from the drugstore)
1/2 teaspoon sugar
1 plastic dishpan or large bowl

Sorting and classifying. Gather four to five each of twelve different things. Mix them up in a bucket and let your child sort them into the compartments of an egg carton. Get these things at the hardware store: 1/2" screws, 1" screws, 1 1/2" screws, small nuts, large nuts, small bolts, large bolts, small metal washers, medium metal washers, large metal washers, plastic washers, and rubber washers. Find these things at home: bobby pins, toothpicks, metal paper clips, plastic paper clips in different sizes and colors, buttons, safety pins, cut up plastic straws, beads, and dried beans. You can vary the collection from time to time to maintain interest.

Counting. Learn the number words in the same way you're learning the alphabet, gradually and with lots of hands-on experiences. Count, count, count. Put numbers in the bottom of an egg carton. Have your child put that number of items in each section.

Supermarket math. When you're shopping, ask your child to get three bars of soap, two packages of cereal, or five cartons of yogurt. At the checkout, always give your child the pennies to count and put in her penny jar. Every now and then let her count 100 pennies and exchange it for a dollar bill (if she's agreeable). Deposit the dollar bill in her savings account and make your trip to the bank a field trip.

Supermarket classification. You can classify what you buy at the supermarket in many different ways: whether you eat it for breakfast, lunch, dinner, snacks, or at any meal; whether you eat it hot or cold; whether it's sweet or sour; whether it's smooth or crunchy; whether it's healthy or junk food; whether it's liquid or solid; whether it's a fruit group, vegetable group, meat group, or bread group; whether it's packaged in paper, plastic, cardboard, aluminum, or tin; whether you can eat it or not eat it; whether it costs under a dollar or over a dollar; and whether it weighs under a pound or over a pound. Naturally you'll only do one classification each time you shop. Before long your child will think of new ways to categorize and classify.

Jar jumble. Save many different sized jars and lids for your child to work with. Match the covers to the jars. Put the jars in order from tallest to shortest or from fattest to thinnest. Use the lids to trace different sized circles with pencil and paper. Fill each jar with a specified number of different objects (e.g. put three marbles in the first jar, three washers in the second jar, three pencils in the third jar, etc.).

Ordering. Help your child understand this concept by playing ordering games from time to time. Line up the blocks from shortest to tallest. Draw pictures of your family starting with tallest to the shortest. Fill several plastic glasses with water and have him arrange them from most to least full.

Thirsty vegetables. Fill an old glass with water. Mix in some red food coloring. Cut off the bottom of an old celery or carrot stick. Let it stand in the water for several hours. Cut open the vegetables and you will find a peppermint striped celery stalk and a bright red carrot. Plants need water just like we do.

Shadow play. Demonstrate to your child that shadows are caused by opaque objects with a light at one side. Both natural and artificial (good concepts to learn) light produce shadows. Have her look for shadows of clouds on fields and water, shadows of trees and buildings, and shadows of people in early morning and late night. Use your flashlight to do shadow animals on the bedroom wall. A good book to accompany your shadow fun is *Shadows: Here, There, and Everywhere* by Ron and Nancy Goor (Thomas Y. Crowell, 1981). There are photographs and easy experiments you can try.

Winter animal fun. Set up a bird feeder and see if you can attract cardinals, bluejays, nuthatches, and chickadees. Visit the zoo in winter when you'll have the place to yourself. Look for animal tracks in the snow (dog, cat, and rabbit are the most common).

Number book. Write the numbers 1 to 10 on individual sheets of paper. Write the words beside the numbers. Cut pictures to place on each page. 1 car, 2 babies, 3 shoes, etc.

Circling numbers. Give your child a red crayon and have her circle all the 1's she can find on a catalog page. Have her circle the 2's in blue, etc.

Number posters. Write the numbers 1 to 10 down the left-hand side of a piece of poster board. Next to each number glue that many objects. You can use raisins, beans, nuts, buttons, sticks, cotton balls, gumdrops, lifesavers, or washers. If your child wants to go on to 20, make a new poster. You can also glue objects in groups of ten which will help your child count in tens. But first master counting to 10.

FIELD TRIPS

In addition to the trips mentioned in Chapters 6 and 7, which are still attractive and inviting to preschoolers, you can plan trips to the following places.

Music store. If you have a music store that displays many different types of instruments, that makes an excellent short field trip for a child. Plan to buy a harmonica while you're there.

Shopping center shows. If you live near a major shopping center, they frequently have special promotional shows to attract shoppers—cars, boats, home improvement, pets, and crafts are all popular subjects. These make quick outings and often present good opportunities for learning.

Sightseeing buses and boat excursions. If you live near a major metropolitan area, there are often sightseeing excursions that are fun. My children have gone on the Wendella Boat Rides on Lake Michigan and found them very exciting.

School and community musical presentations. Many communities have children's theater presentations that make wonderful field trips for preschoolers. We have enjoyed *Charlotte's Web*, *Cinderella*, and *The Wizard of Oz*, all given by our local drama club. Watch your local paper for inexpensive productions such as these.

Small and large airports. To the preschooler fascinated with air travel, a visit to an airport is a must. A smaller airport will usually afford you a much closer view of airplanes and you might even talk a friendly worker into letting you see an airplane up close. I have given up driving to O'Hare International Airport; all family members who fly now take buses back and forth. But when my children were very small, we flew to Grandma's house and that was quite an adventure.

School. Visit your local school so your child can begin to imagine herself as a student there. Perhaps you know a child who attends now and can visit a classroom or the library. At the very least, walk around the outside of the building on a weekend and peek in classrooms. Play on the playground and talk with your child about all of the fun she will have at school.

Museums. Living as we do in a suburb of Chicago, we are especially fortunate to be within driving distance of three major museums: The Art Institute of Chicago, The Museum of Science and Industry, and The Field Museum of Natural History. All of these institutions have displays and exhibits that are geared to young children, and we have visited them all. Older preschoolers will benefit most from such field trips, particularly if you have to drive any distance to reach them.

Now that your preschooler is almost ready for school, don't stop the learning fun. Many of the ideas presented in this chapter will provide family fun for years to come. As your child grows to maturity, he will begin to come up with his own activities, experiments, and projects that are even better than anything in the preceding chapters. Then you'll know that you've done a terrific job!

What Every Parent Is Afraid to Ask

CHAPTER NINE

Preschool and School Success

I WISH I COULD SAY I SENT MY DAUGHTER to preschool for academic enrichment. Or even social development. I wish I could say I carefully evaluated a number of options and selected the one that best met my child's needs. Alas, none of the above is true.

At the time I enrolled Emily in the Sunshine Preschool at the Wheaton Evangelical Free Church, I was desperate for a couple of mornings with only one child to manage. It was affordable and had openings after the school year had started.

But we were especially blessed. Mrs. Tobais was a warm and caring teacher. There was just the right mix of learning and fun. Stories and songs, free play, and finger painting—each day was filled with fun. Best of all, Emily made new friends and had a chance to be on her own without an overprotective mother.

Everywhere I go, parents have questions about preschools. Stay-at-home moms wonder if preschool is necessary at all. They feel societal pressure to make sure their children do not fall behind their counterparts who have been in formal schooling for several years, but they value the time they spend with their children and want to savor it for just a little longer. They sometimes feel the financial burden of preschool will overload an already thinly stretched budget.

Those working parents whose children are already in day-care are eager to find a more stimulating environment for their child, whether it be an academic preschool, a Montessori school, a church nursery school, or a play group. Both sets of parents are deeply concerned about their children's intellectual, social, and emotional development and want the very best for their children. They just aren't sure what the best really is.

IS PRESCHOOL ESSENTIAL TO MY CHILD'S ACADEMIC SUCCESS?

Absolutely not! Preschools for three and four year olds are not essential. A cooperative home play group or a weekly Sunday school experience can provide many of the same experiences found in preschool. But unfortunately, many of today's young parents have much higher expectations than just "fun and games" for their children before they enter kindergarten. They want high powered academic programs that will insure success in later life. They are rushing their children to grow up fast so they can become independent and self-sufficient.

However, forcing independence and self-sufficiency on very young children will have exactly the opposite effect from that intended. A highly structured, competitive atmosphere can be detrimental to many children; experiencing failure before one has the social and emotional skills to handle it can be devastating. David Elkind, in his powerful book *Miseducation: Preschoolers at Risk*, said it best: "Early childhood is a very important period of life. It is a period when children learn an enormous amount about the everyday world. It is also the time during which young children acquire lifelong attitudes toward themselves, toward others, and toward academic learning. But it is not the time for formal academic instruction."[1]

THEN WHAT IS THE PURPOSE OF PRESCHOOL?

Beware of preschools that send home worksheets and claim to teach your child how to read. Beware of preschools that promise educational gains and readiness for school. Beware of class lessons that focus on group drill and emphasize rote

160

memory. Developmentally, only a small percentage of children show readiness for reading instruction before the age of six, and even those precocious children do best without formal instruction.

Preschools that focus on "instruction" are teacher centered. Preschools should be child centered and provide the same types of activities and learning experiences found in Chapters 6, 7, and 8. In an ideal preschool, the focus is on creative play. Stories and songs are a part of each day. There is an ample supply of arts and crafts materials, and children are encouraged to create their own products, not follow a pattern. Preschools should give children an opportunity to play and learn with other children in a low-key and unstructured way.

How Can I Tell One Preschool from Another?

As you begin your search for just the right preschool, here are some general categories to help organize your choices:

- *Private preschool.* Usually owned by an individual, the private school offers half-day programs for three and four year olds. Montessori Schools are usually privately owned.

- *Church-affiliated preschool.* With a curriculum based on some religious education, the programs are usually half-day and geared to both three and four year olds

- *Parents' cooperative.* A preschool formed by a group of parents who hire the teacher. Usually only one class is held and parents frequently participate as aides. A variation on this theme has different parents serving as teachers during different periods of the year.

- *Commercial or franchised school.* Sometimes held in conjunction with a franchised day-care center. Often promises a high level of early learning.

- *Day-care center.* Many day-care centers have included an educational component into their program.

- *Head Start or public school programs.* These programs are usually compensatory or remedial in nature and serve children who appear to be at risk because of their family or developmental background.
- *College or university lab preschool.* These provide a training ground for students and often serve as models for preschools in general.

DOES EACH PRESCHOOL HAVE A DIFFERENT KIND OF PROGRAM?

Although there are many different types of preschools, there are really only three basic philosophies that prevail: the traditional preschool, academic preschool, and Montessori preschool.

- The traditional preschool or American nursery school, as it once was called, is characterized by free play and discovery learning. Teachers in the traditional preschool believe that children can make decisions about their learning and leave them free to explore and discover in an out-of-home setting.
- The academic preschool focuses on the development of pre-reading and pre-math skills and does so through direct instruction. Content is taught by teachers rather than being informally discovered and learned by students.
- The Montessori Schools, although there are many variations on Maria Montessori's original theme, are based on the concept of order. There are many specially developed materials for learning, and children are permitted to choose and make decisions about what they will learn and do within the framework of materials available. Three categories of materials are used: those to develop competence in daily activities such as washing, sweeping, peeling; those to develop sensory skills, such as blocks, beads, shapes; and those that teach the academic skills of mathematics and reading.

When you visit the traditional, academic, and Montessori schools, you will no doubt find many similarities between them. Often what is actually happening in classrooms is different from what the director or the brochure may say. It may be that you will have a difficult time deciding just which philosophy is espoused. Talk with the teachers, observe for an extended period, and talk to parents of students already enrolled. They will probably be your best source of information about what is actually happening on a daily basis.

WHAT ELSE SHOULD I LOOK FOR WHEN I VISIT?

The National Academy of Early Childhood Programs has developed a checklist for parents to use in evaluating preschool and day-care programs. Here are some of the items they feel are important:

1. Are you welcome to visit the facility at any time and to become involved in the program so you can become knowledgeable about and comfortable with your child's environment?

2. Is there open communication with parents about potential difficulties, concerns, and positive experiences as staff and parents work together as a team?

3. Are the teachers friendly and accepting, helping each child feel valued?

4. Do the teachers help children resolve conflicts independently?

5. Is discipline fair, kind, and reasonable? Are limits and expectations of appropriate behavior clearly expressed?

6. Are the children happy and involved, interacting positively and frequently with each other and the teachers?

7. Are the children provided with opportunities for decision-making and problem-solving?

8. Are children encouraged to have hands-on participation with freedom of choice?

9. Are abundant materials within easy reach for children to enjoy both on a one-to-one and small group basis?

10. Are books plentiful, easily accessible, of fine quality, and developmentally geared?

11. Do activities provide opportunities with a balance of active/quiet, indoor/outdoor, individual/group, large muscle/small muscle experiences?

12. Is the emphasis on the process of the children's involvement rather than on a finished product to impress parents?

13. Do caregivers demonstrate respect for cultural differences?

14. Are spaces provided for block building, dramatic play, art, music, and a quiet book corner?

15. Does the playground have areas for large motor activities (swings, climbing apparatus) as well as creative construction (blocks, boards, boxes, paint, water) with both hard and soft surfaces for play?

16. Are the bathrooms sized right and clean, with functional faucets, paper towels, and soap?

17. Is the environment cheerful and inviting?

18. Is the equipment well maintained and age-appropriate?

19. Is the center licensed by the appropriate agencies?

20. Is the staff qualified, having had child-care training and experience?[2]

If you only have time to evaluate one thing, make sure it's the teacher. She (and sometimes he) is the most important part of your child's preschool experience. My children still talk of Mrs. Tobias with reverence. She made them feel special and loved. What she taught was incidental to who she was.

1. Elkind, David. *Miseducation: Preschoolers at Risk*, Alfred A. Knopf, New York, 1987, p. 71.

2. Shiff, Eileen, Ed. *Experts Advise Parents*, New York, Delacorte, 1987, pp. 348-351.

CHAPTER TEN

Can I Do It All?

Working and Preschoolers

Donna and Chuck are successful young professionals. They juggle careers, children, home, and community involvement in a veritable whirlwind of activity. The secret of their success was Dorothy, a grandmother who had raised her own family. She provided in-home care for Jenny and Elizabeth, their preschool daughters. In addition to child care, Dorothy did some light cleaning, put dinner in the oven, and even threw a load of clothes in the washing machine now and then. Dorothy was more than just a baby-sitter. She read stories, took the girls on shopping excursions, and served cookies and milk after preschool. Donna was secure in the knowledge that her children and her home were in good hands.

Then the bubble burst. Dorothy decided to take an office job. The well organized and secure environment that Dorothy helped to create was thrust into chaos. Jenny and Elizabeth were devastated; Dorothy had been with them as long as they could remember. Donna was depressed. She wasn't able to find anyone to take Dorothy's place in her home and had to turn to outside day care. Chuck was frantic. Gone were the hot meals and clean house he had come to expect. Donna and Chuck are still putting the pieces back together.

Marlene, recently divorced and the mother of a two-year-old, faces another dilemma. Although Jesse loves his in-home day-care setting, he is especially susceptible to the illnesses that pass back and forth between children. For him a simple cold often turns into a life-threatening illness. Marlene's mother has been a godsend. When Jesse needs to regain his strength after an especially bad bout of bronchitis, she leaves her home in a nearby city and spends the time nursing him back to health. Juggling trips to the doctor and hospital while working in a competitive engineering position has become a way of life for Marlene. The question is, can she hold on until Jesse outgrows his health problems?

Marlene and Donna face the major problems associated with being a working mother on a daily basis. Whether yours is a two-career family or a single parent family, the challenges of raising children, especially preschoolers, while working are formidable. In addition to facing fatigue and frustration, these young mothers are also plagued by anxiety and guilt.

WHAT ARE THE IMPORTANT QUESTIONS TO ASK?

Here are some things you might want to consider if you are contemplating making a decision to work full-time while raising infants, toddlers, or preschoolers.

1. *Do I have the option of job-sharing, working at home, or part-time employment?*

I know of many young women who have creatively managed to blend their careers and families. A lawyer in my neighborhood stopped commuting to the city after her first child was born, but continued to handle local cases for her firm on a contract basis. A music teacher in our district shares her job with another young mother. Together they each have time for family and career. I began tutoring students while staying at home with my children. My editor moved her computer to a home office and edits while her youngest is in preschool.

2. *Have I visited a family day-care home or group day-care center and spent at least one or two full days observing what goes on? Could I leave my child in this environment with comfort and ease?*

Finding the right kind of day care will make the difference between success and failure as a working parent. Marlene interviewed thirty-nine in-home day-care providers before settling on one. She was searching for a warm, loving, intelligent family environment. In over three dozen tries, she only found one home that met her requirements. Don't settle for less than the very best in care for your child.

3. *Am I working for primarily economic reasons, or are personal satisfaction and career advancement the major considerations?*

Making the decision to be a working mom of very young children is never easy. But take the time and thought that is needed to make the right decision for you.

4. *Do I have the organizational skills and maturity to handle a full time job and parenting?*

Doing a good job of both parenting and working requires an exceptional level of organization and maturity. Perhaps that is why many couples today delay having children until their late twenties or thirties. They are established in careers and have built up a work record that stands them in good stead when they need time off for family emergencies, and have the maturation and coping skills to live with the high-stress lifestyle that accompanies working while parenting.

WHEN TO GO BACK TO WORK AFTER YOU HAVE A BABY

T. Berry Brazelton, in his encouraging book *Working and Caring*, suggests four different stages in the infant-parent relationship which are important to the process of attachment. These stages, which last through four months of age, are crucial to the development of communication and understanding between the infant and parent. Brazelton suggests that a mother be at home for this four-month period if at all possible. He also suggests that a father have some time at home. According to Dr. Brazelton, parents need to get through the crucial fourth month, when babies usually begin to settle into a routine, so they can feel successful and connected to their newborn.

Burton L. White, Director for the Center of Parent Education, is not as supportive of "other care" for children under the age of thirty months. He emphatically states: "Day care simply is not in the best interest of children under thirty months of age. Beyond six months of age, substitute care should be limited to no more than three to four hours a day, five days a week, for the balance of the first two-and-a half years."[1]

DAY CARE OR BABY-SITTER: WHICH IS BETTER?

My first choice for child care is someone who will come to your home and care for your children in their own environment. But "Dorothys" are usually expensive and hard to find. The next best choice, in my opinion, is in-home child care. Another mother who is caring for her own child and one or two others can provide a pleasant social group and does not introduce the institutionalized atmosphere of commercial day-care centers. Even better is a grandmother or parent of older children whose own toddlers or preschoolers are not competing with your children for her attention.

My last choice is the commercial daycare center, for obvious reasons. Low salaries and frequent turnover in many of these centers make them unattractive for the very young child.

FOSTERING WELL-ROUNDED DEVELOPMENT IN CHILDREN

What are the most important things working parents can do to ensure that their children are well-developed? Here's what some working moms of preschoolers interviewed for this book had to say:

- "Relax and laugh with your child as much as possible. Leave stress at work. Children pick up so quickly on stress, and they should learn that work doesn't always make parents unhappy. Also, if given the chance, children are great at cheering up adults and reminding us of the simple joys!"

- "When you are tired, remember to stay patient. Keep your rules with your children even though you may feel guilty because you haven't seen them all day. Even though you may have housework to

do, spend time with your kids, playing, reading, and coloring with them."
- "Find a Christian environment, whether it's in a private home or in daycare."
- "Be consistent. Be a loving but firm disciplinarian."
- "Be organized. Spend quality time each day and make sure it is the same time each day."

STAYING ON AN EVEN KEEL

What are some of the most important things working moms can do to keep their own lives from getting out of control?
- "Keep everything in its proper perspective. Remember that family comes first. Your children need you and those years will slip by and never return."
- "Make your time together good "quality time" for they are young for such a short time. The house doesn't have to be perfect. Make weekends special."
- "If possible, try for some 'irregularity' in your schedule. Try working three days and two evenings or having one afternoon off. Try thirty-five hours rather than forty. It makes an incredible difference in family morale, but not much difference in the paycheck."
- "Don't try to do it all. Get help from outside or from your husband."
- "Try to be organized. Let the housework go if you're feeling bogged down."
- "Keep calm. Don't take your frustrations out on your children. Keep yourself organized. It makes your life easier and your children happier."
- "It is hard being a working parent. It is also hard on children. If you have a bad day, stop and think before you pick them up. Don't make your child's life so rigid that it makes him a nervous wreck. He is only a child."

WHAT ARE THE BENEFITS OF WORKING?

Although working mothers face many difficulties and challenges, there are many benefits that accrue to their children as a result of their parents' careers. When working parents are in the middle of the Pampers and the peanut butter, they seldom have time to reflect on the positive aspects of working parenthood, but there are many.

As the parent of two successful teenagers, I can look back and see that their independence, self-reliance, and feelings of self-worth and competence began as I gave them responsibilities and opportunities at home because I was a working parent. In my opinion, these benefits accrue only if parents are not feeling guilty, fatigued, frustrated, and overworked as a result of their dual responsibilities.

- "Working mothers provide healthy role models for their children. What better place for children to learn how to handle a variety of jobs at the same time while maintaining cool and composure? What better way for children to learn how to set priorities and get organized? Working moms have a wonderful opportunity to model and teach as they fulfill their multiple roles."

- "Working mothers are often happier because their needs for self-fulfillment are being met. I know that my own interest in learning and growing has been fueled in my workplace. I try to think of those benefits when there isn't any clean underwear, the dishwasher is broken, and I forgot to take anything out of the freezer for dinner."

- "Working mothers raise children who are independent and self-motivated. Moms who are independent and self-motivated just naturally inspire those qualities in their children. We can talk more eloquently about doing homework if we have a little of our own to do from time to time. If we're always available to meet every need and solve every problem, our children will never have an opportunity to 'try their own wings.'"

- "Working mothers don't meddle and get overinvolved in their children's day-to-day problems. I know my children were forced to handle minor emergencies and solve problems in very productive ways because I wasn't always there to 'hold their hands.' Of course we need to be available for emergencies, but everyone's definition of an emergency is different. If you forget your lunch and know Mom can't bring you one, you become resourceful about asking to share someone else's and then definitely remembering yours tomorrow."

WHAT ARE THE BIGGEST PROBLEMS WORKING PARENTS FACE?

Working moms of preschoolers face a unique set of problems. Their children often cannot verbalize their frustrations and concerns. Sleepless nights and frequent illnesses often plague the early years as well. The working moms of preschoolers spoke eloquently of their frustrations and fears.

Problems with their children's well-being:

- "Illnesses! The children at day care pass illnesses back and forth all winter long. Then we pass the cold among ourselves for a few weeks. My child seems to be on antibiotics almost all winter. We all miss good health. Juggling work with trips to the doctor every week or so while constantly fighting off colds ourselves is difficult."

- "There's extra stress when I'm absent from work due to my child's illness."

- "I feel guilty when my child is sick and I have to leave her with someone else."

- "Deciding when to take off work when your children are sick is difficult. I feel guilty when I take them to day care and they're not feeling up to par."

Problems with the constant rush to get everything done:

- "Dropping two children off at different places is difficult. One is in day care and the other is in preschool."

- "There's never enough time to do it all."

- "Getting out the door without confrontations is really hard."

Problems with lack of time to spend with children:

- "Lack of time to spend with my child during the week is hard. I feel 'quality time' is a myth. I am tired and short of patience by the end of the day. The other problem is not knowing what is going on at the sitter's or school."
- "Morning rush out the door and the evening hassle of getting dinner!"
- "There's not enough time to spend with my children. My job involves many evening meetings also, which is very hard for my children to understand."

Problems with the guilt that plagues all working moms:

- "Guilt! The sense that there isn't enough time to do any task well. I feel like I'm doing a half-baked job of being a mom, wife, church member, employee, and friend."
- "The guilt from leaving them and not knowing everything they've done. Either they don't remember or they can't express themselves clearly enough to tell me."
- "I love my job and could put hours into it if I didn't have so many other responsibilities. It's hard to be a perfect mother/wife/homemaker/ hostess/friend/worker."

SO HOW DO WORKING MOMS COPE?

In spite of the challenges and frustrations, working moms survive. Marlene put it this way: "There are many tactless co-workers who make comments such as 'You should be home with your child like a good mother.' Occasionally I have doubts as to whether I am doing the right thing, but most of the time I just look at how well adjusted and bright my son is, and I know I'm doing fine."

How do they do it? Here's what the working moms I interviewed told me:

1. Organize, organize, organize.
   - "I lay everything out the night before. Any unexpected event can ruin the routine and make you late."

- "Pack up the car the night before!"
- "Prepare and freeze dinners on the weekends or do a double batch during the week."
- "Make lists for errands and chores that need doing."
- "Lay out everyone's clothes, backpacks, and brief-cases the night before. Have lunches made, labelled, and in the refrigerator for easy pickup in the morning."
- "When I see something on sale that will make a good birthday present, I buy several, wrap them, and store them until the next party invitation arrives."

2. Delegate, delegate, delegate.
- "Everybody contributes to keeping the family running smoothly. Mom, Dad, and children all do their part."
- "My husband feeds the children breakfast while I get ready for work."
- "If you can afford a cleaning woman, hire one! If you can't, lower your standards."

3. Prioritize, prioritize, prioritize.
- "If I'm cooking dinner, my preschooler is helping me. She does simple jobs to help and we make a game out of it. I'm having fun while getting a critical job done."
- "I set aside ten to fifteen minutes daily at the same time every day (except on weekends) to work with my child. We read, play games, and learn something new. Bedtime seems to be the best time for this. My children (four of them) seem to remember best the things I teach them before bedtime."
- "We play games in the car—singing songs, rhyming words, and finding colors. Each trip we take we look for a different color."
- "If I'm tired after a long day, we lie on the floor on our backs, each with a flashlight, dim the

> lights, and play games. We chase each other's
> beams and write on the ceiling."

Don't be concerned with fancy dinners, folded laundry, and an immaculate household. Have fun! You'll have plenty of time for gourmet cooking and ironed underwear when your children are older.

THE IMPACT OF WORKING MOTHERS

Conventional wisdom in the pediatric community as late as 1978 held that women should put their careers on hold until their children were at least three years or older. Many felt that some sort of maternal deprivation would occur if mother wasn't there on a regular basis. This belief continues to haunt many a working mother and creates an underlying feeling of guilt and distress that can only further depress the stressed-out working mother.

But pediatric opinion has shifted its views more recently to keep pace with a new body of research that shows infants can bond with their mothers while also enjoying relationships with other caretakers. The critical variable is the behavior and continuity of the primary caretaker. Research has demonstrated the importance of certain child-rearing behaviors (see earlier chapters) and the primary caretaker must exhibit skills in these areas for optimum child development.

Children can readily adapt to a variety of caretakers, but if there are too many and if they keep changing too frequently, the predictability that is so important in a child's life will vanish. Herein lies the dilemma of working moms—where to find that ideal caretaker. Marlene had to interview thirty-nine before she found the right one. Donna and Chuck had just the right one, but she quit. I'm afraid that many of us do not have the fortitude and energy to deal with the challenges of finding the ideal caretaker, but we dare not ever leave our children with less than the best.

Working moms are quick to assume every problem they encounter in child rearing can be laid at the doorstep of their career status. As I reflect on the problems I faced as a young mother with illnesses, toilet training, temper tantrums, eating problems, and guilt, I must remind working moms to network with their stay-at-home counterparts once in awhile. They may be pleased to discover that a problem they blamed on their working status is common to all young children.

SOURCES OF ADDITIONAL INFORMATION

Working parents need all the help and encouragement they can get. If you would like to read more about this topic, there are many excellent books that will give you more detailed information. Books that are out of print can be obtained from your public library. Books with a Christian emphasis are designated with an asterisk.

THE DAY CARE DILEMMA (Marian Blum, D.C. Heath, 1983)—Must reading for anyone who is considering placing a child in a daycare center. Good discussion of the political and moral ramifications of day care as a national problem.

WORKING AND CARING (T. Berry Brazelton, M.D., Addison-Wesley, 1985)—Brazelton once again demonstrates why he is such a popular writer with parents. He is warm, understanding, and intelligent. His case studies give the working parent an opportunity to "peek in" on how other families are coping. Somehow knowing that others are going through the same situations—and surviving—is comforting.

THE SINGLE MOTHER'S HANDBOOK (Elizabeth S. Greywolf, William Morrow and Company, 1984)—Single mothers have the most challenging job that I know of. My hat is off to them. I work with them as parents in my school, and they are courageous and resourceful. This book is a good resource for all areas of the single mother's life, including discussion of children's health, nutrition, and day care.

50/50 PARENTING (Gayle Kimball, Lexington Books, 1988)—For couples committed to changing the traditional "mother does it all" life-style, this book will be a blessing.

*WORKING MOTHERS** (Kay Kuzma, Stratford Press, 1981)—Practical suggestions for coping with the stresses of being a working mother.

THE PARENTS' GUIDE TO DAYCARE (Jo Ann Miller and Susan Weissman, Bantam, 1986)—Information the working parent will need in order to make intelligent choices about daycare is provided in this volume. There are lots of interesting anecdotes about "real" children that will help you envision your child in a daycare setting.

HOW TO HAVE A CHILD AND KEEP YOUR JOB (Jane Price, St. Martin's Press, 1979)—Addresses some critical issues such as how your job could affect your child's development and the reality of "quality time."

WHEN OTHERS CARE FOR YOUR CHILD (Time-Life Books, Inc., 1987)—Although disconcerting to the working parent, this discussion on the debate over daycare featuring T. Berry Brazelton, Burton L. White, Ellen Galinsky, Jay Belsky, and other early childhood specialists is valuable.

*SHOULD YOU BE THE WORKING MOM?** (Bee-Lan C. Wang and Richard J. Stellway, David C. Cook Publishing Co., 1987)—Help in making the decision and living with the results. Here is a practical book that takes the myths out of the working mom. Based on extensive research.

1. Time-Life Books, Inc. *When Others Care for Your Child*, Time-Life, 1987, p. 17.

CHAPTER ELEVEN

Off to School: Ready or Not

THE SUMMER BEFORE EMILY WENT OFF to kindergarten was an anxious time for me. We'd received word at kindergarten registration in the spring: your child must know how to tie her shoes before she enters kindergarten. The class had a daily gym period, and the gym teacher was adamant. Each student must wear gym shoes to class and then remove them after gym to hang them on his or her chair. This was serious business, and I was sure they would turn Emily away at the door if she could not demonstrate her proficiency at once. But no matter how diligently I tried, she wasn't willing to learn.

Fortunately for me, Alice came along. Alice had just received her degree in early childhood education and did some baby-sitting for us that summer. Emily and Alice had a special affinity, and within a few days Emily was practicing her shoelace tying with enthusiasm and success. In the nick of time, she had mastered the only prerequisite for entrance to Whittier School's kindergarten.

With the invention of Velcro, shoelaces are no longer a problem for the average kindergarten student. But there are other more significant skills that are critical for success. While conducting one of my frequent observations in the kindergarten class, I notice that everyone is listening to Mrs. Williams read a story—except Steven. He is playing with

Amy's braids. During the discussion, Steven doesn't raise his hand. He has found a piece of scrap paper on the floor and is tearing it up into little pieces. Mrs. Williams calls his name and tries to engage his attention to the class activity but with little success. During the free play period, while a group of boys is building a ramp for their cars and trucks, Steven wanders from group to group. He seems unable to focus on a specific activity or get involved in a project. I ask the kindergarten teacher about him. Her answer is simple, "I don't think Steven is ready for kindergarten. He's one of the youngest children in the class."

Kindergarten readiness is a much discussed and debated topic. State legislatures have rolled back entrance dates to give children the benefit of several more months of growth and development. Many school districts have even instituted pre-kindergarten testing to determine if a child is indeed ready for school.

In the sections ahead, you will find answers to the most often asked questions about kindergarten readiness and several checklists to help you determine if your child is "ready."

WHAT DOES RESEARCH TELL US?

Research says that the older children in a class do better academically and socially than their younger counterparts.[1] And these differences between the youngest and oldest children in a classroom group do not disappear as they move along in elementary school. A study of children with summer birthdays who had and had not entered school after turning five compared the two groups at third grade and at sixth grade. Among the boys who had delayed their entrance into kindergarten, seventy-nine percent had above-average grades, compared to only twenty-seven percent in the early entrance group. Among girls, seventy-one percent of the delayed entrants had above-average grades, compared to only twenty-two percent for the early entrants.[2]

WHAT DOES A TYPICAL KINDERGARTEN STUDENT LOOK LIKE?

The following checklist describes an *average* child about to enter kindergarten. You will notice that both positive and negative descriptors are used. Please remember that your child will not correspond in every area—there isn't a child alive who exhibits every one of these characteristics. However, if your child differs significantly, consult with your pediatrician, preschool teacher, or other educational professional about the possibility of delaying kindergarten entrance.

SOCIAL DEVELOPMENT

- selects friends
- demonstrates sensitivity to others
- comforts playmates when they are upset
- enjoys interacting with four to five children without continual supervision
- has difficulty distinguishing fantasy from reality
- thinks about ideas and designs own projects and dramatic play
- explores a variety of roles through creative play
- dramatizes sections of stories
- cooperates in group games, following rules
- adds to adult conversation
- works independently for twenty to thirty minutes
- takes turns with groups of other children
- enjoys competition in play
- behaves erratically
- makes surly faces and talks back when denied something he wants
- prefers to play in groups
- becomes overbearing and negative at times
- enjoys showing off
- is sometimes physically and verbally aggressive
- sometimes attacks with name calling
- is sometimes careless and destructive with toys
- enjoys telling "tall tales"

COGNITIVE DEVELOPMENT

- identifies first, middle, and last position
- counts by rote from one to twenty
- names a part of a picture that is missing, is inappropriate, or that doesn't belong

- matches one-to-one when manipulating ten items
- understands the concepts of behind, beside, next to
- understands the concepts of long and short
- stacks ten blocks in imitation of a pyramid
- draws a man with a head, a trunk, and four limbs
- identifies color of a given object
- matches letters and numbers
- knows eight colors
- names the missing object when it is removed from a group of three
- describes objects as light or heavy
- enjoys rhyming words and repeats familiar rhymes
- tells when during the day certain activities occur
- remembers four objects seen in a picture
- reproduces a triangle
- names five textures
- sorts objects
- follows a series of three directions
- pairs objects together
- employs compound sentences
- identifies top and bottom of objects
- uses contractions
- is interested in world beyond home and school
- enjoys questioning
- uses imagination creatively
- describes opposites using analogies
- relates familiar story without picture clues

PHYSICAL DEVELOPMENT
- dresses independently
- cuts two-inch circles
- draws representational pictures (house, man, tree)
- pastes and cuts simple shapes
- cuts along a curved line
- copies a cross and a square
- prints name in capital letters
- swings independently, pumping by himself
- balances on one foot four to eight seconds

- changes directions while running
- walks across balance beam
- hops backward with both feet
- plays bounce and catch with a big ball
- walks down stairs, using alternate feet
- maneuvers tricycle around corners
- can hop on one foot five successive times

WHAT A CHILD SHOULD KNOW

You can't give children a crash course in "kindergarten" to get them ready. Most of the things they should know before they begin will have been learned in a gradual way during the first five years of life. But if you uncover a small deficiency, perhaps a bit of practice will help.

There are two categories of things to know: survival information and academic information. The former is essential to success in kindergarten, but you needn't worry if your children have some gaps in the second category. They'll have plenty of time to learn these things in kindergarten.

SURVIVAL INFORMATION

- how to button, zip, tie, and get in and out of clothing
- know full name (not just nickname)
- know house number, street, and phone number (if not, tuck in shirt pocket)
- know parents' first and last names
- are prepared for length of time away (clock)
- know the way to and from school
- have broken in new shoes ahead of time
- know bus routines (simple rules about staying in seat)
- know how to put things in and take them out of back pack
- care for themselves at toilet without help
- wash their own hands and face
- make their wants known in short, simple sentences
- play reasonably well with other children
- listen quietly while being read a short story or poem

ACADEMIC INFORMATION

- count to ten
- count objects
- name colors
- recite the alphabet
- cut with scissors
- draw a man
- copy a square
- print name
- understand opposites (heavy/light, hot/cold, up/down)

WHAT WILL MY CHILD LEARN IN KINDERGARTEN?

Again, don't worry if your children don't measure up to every readiness checklist you've consulted. No child has every skill developed to the same level of expertise. You will be amazed at how your children will grow and change in the short space of nine months away from you.

In addition to all of the social and emotional development that takes place during the year, kindergarten students learn in the areas of visual skills, auditory skills, gross motor skills, language skills, and fine motor skills.

You may feel that your children already know everything they'll learn in kindergarten. Don't be too sure. Experienced and skillful kindergarten teachers are masters at identifying those areas where children still need help and designing activities that enhance them.

Here are the specific skills that will be learned:

Visual Skills (What do they see? How do they interpret it?) Games and activities that teach colors, shapes, sizes, numerals, and upper- and lower-case letters are all designed to sharpen children's visual skills.

Auditory Skills (What do they hear? How do they interpret it?) Children will learn to listen without interrupting, follow simple directions, identify differences in verbal and nonverbal sounds, recognize rhyming words, listen and retell a story, repeat a series (4, 6, 1), and recognize beginning sounds.

Gross Motor Skills (How do they move their bodies during a given task?) Children will develop an awareness and skill in many large motor activities like: walking, skipping, galloping, running, hopping, throwing, and catching. They will also learn to direct their bodies in different directions like left and right.

Language Skills (How do they express themselves and understand the concepts of their environment?) Children will continue to learn to express themselves with words and sentences in order to communicate with those around them. They will do this through pronouncing words correctly, expressing themselves in complete sentences, communicating with their peer group in complete sentences using correct words, enlarging their vocabulary, telling stories in sequence, counting and applying numerals, identifying concepts such as tall, high, and long, and identifying opposites such as up and down.

Fine Motor Skills (How do they interact with objects using their hands?) Children will refine their awareness and development of small muscle activity through manipulating small objects, cutting, holding crayons and pencils properly, drawing lines, shapes and forms, and forming letters and numerals.

KINDERGARTEN SCREENING AND PRE-TESTING

A lot of people wish they knew a little more about the test their child will be given when he is ready for kindergarten. If you'll promise not to administer this test to your children yourself, I'll include a copy for your information. But first, another caveat. Don't be alarmed if your child can't count to twenty or give an answer to why we have clocks. This is a screening device, and it is designed so that a certain number of questions are extremely difficult.

If you are determined to have the information, let someone else administer the test. Children frequently balk at performing on cue for parents, and an impartial test administrator will more likely achieve a greater degree of cooperation from your child.

DEVELOPMENTAL TASKS

I. Gross Motor

- A. Hop on one foot four times in place.
- B. Skip four steps
- C. Balance on each foot alternately with eyes open for ten seconds. Do same task with eyes closed for four seconds.
- D. Walk three yards on toes without touching heels to floor.
- E. Walk backward three steps.
- F. Catch a large ball at a distance of six feet.
- G. Throw a tennis ball a distance of six feet—with right hand, with left hand.
- H. Sight on fixed object through rolled paper—with right eye, with left eye.

II. Cognitive Verbal

- A. Count from 1 to 20. (Observer notes numerals and order.)
- B. Reproduce model. (Observer builds three steps with six blocks, then asks child to do the same six inches from model.)
- C. Count objects. (Observer places three blocks on table and asks child how many blocks there are.)
- D. Identify colors: red, white, blue, black, green, yellow.
- E. Recognize and name five or more letters on a printed page of large type.
- F. Read a short sentence.

III. Fine Motor

- A. Reproduce folded paper model. (Observer folds 6″ x 6″ paper diagonally, then folds it in half. Hands child another piece of paper to fold like model.)
- B. Touch thumbs to four fingers on both hands.
- C. Copy letters D, N, E from model. (Observer does not demonstrate).
- D. Cut four-inch circle with scissors to within one-eighth of an inch of the line—with right hand, with left hand.

E. Color four-inch square within the lines—with right hand, with left hand.

OTHER ABILITIES—In addition to checking the child's ability to handle the previous developmental tasks, the screening may include language and speech checks.

A. Language comprehension (Can he follow simple directions?)
B. Auditory sequential memory (Can he repeat a series of digits back to you?)
C. Analogies (Fire is hot. Ice is_____.)
D. Story sequencing (Tell a brief story and ask child to repeat it.)
E. Same/Different (Which picture is not like the others?)
F. Why (Questions about why we take a bath or why we have clocks)
G. Articulation (How does the child pronounce words, how fluid is his speech?)
H. Vocabulary (Child is given series of words and needs to know their meanings.)[3]

WHAT IF MY CHILD IS NOT "READY" FOR KINDERGARTEN?

If you reach the conclusion that your child is not quite ready for kindergarten, you have some options. Do not be hesitant to exercise them.

Your first option is to wait a year before sending your child to kindergarten. Louise Bates Ames, in her book *Is Your Child in the Wrong Grade?*, states that at least half of the school failures in first grade could be prevented if children started school only when they were fully ready. She believes that children should be started in school (and subsequently promoted) on the basis of their behavioral age and not their chronological age.

If your child is among the oldest in the class rather than the youngest, his chances of experiencing success improve dramatically. Of course, if you continually discuss his "failure" in front of Grandma, Aunt Minnie, and the mailman, elaborating on the reasons for your decision, you may defeat the purpose of giving your child the self-confidence and extra maturity he needs.

A second option available to parents is enrolling a child in a private school where the curriculum and/or teaching style may be more appropriate to the child's developmental level.

A third option is to home school your child. If you've already created an optimum learning environment in your home by collecting the materials and following the suggestions given earlier in the book, then becoming your child's formal teacher will be a relatively simple matter. You'll no doubt want to develop a more comprehensive philosophy and curriculum to comply with the educational standards of your state, but just continue doing what you've been doing for five or six years—making learning fun.

HOW CAN I HELP MAKE THE FIRST DAY OF SCHOOL A SUCCESS?

As the start of school approaches, here are some things you can do to prepare your child for the adventure that lies ahead of him.

- Visit the school and classroom ahead of time. If possible, meet the teacher, principal, librarian, and other important school personnel. Walk through the halls and play on the playground. You will want your child to feel comfortable and at home on the first day.

- Let your child wear familiar clothes and shoes on the first day of school. You will be tempted to dress him in a handsome fall outfit, but the first day of school is often a scorcher. Let your child choose what he wants to wear.

- Find out what a typical day in kindergarten is like and talk about it ahead of time. Use dolls or puppets to act out what will happen during the school day.

- Find out what school supplies are needed in kindergarten and go shopping together for them. Allow your child to choose the folders and pencils he will use.

- A few days before school starts, practice getting up in the morning and getting ready. Decide whether you will eat breakfast first or get dressed first. Choose a special place to lay out your child's backpack. It's never too early to start getting organized.
- Talk with your child about what you will be doing while he is in school. Let him visit your workplace or show him the gym where you will be working out while he is in school. If you will be at home taking care of younger siblings, reassure him that you will miss him while he is at school.
- On the first day of school, get up about thirty minutes early to make sure you have enough time for all of the last-minute preparations.
- If your child will walk to school, practice the route he will take for several days before school begins. You may accompany him on the first day, but if you are a working parent, he may walk with other students or with a sitter. Talk about the familiar landmarks along the way.
- Make sure that you have all of the immunization and physical examination forms completed before school begins. In many districts, students are excluded if all of the paperwork is not in order.
- If your child will ride the bus, see if you can climb aboard a school bus and see what it feels like to sit in the seats.
- Talk about feelings your child may have. Acknowledge that he may be fearful or nervous. Talk about how you feel in new situations and what you do to overcome those feelings.
- Read a book about the first day of school. Here are some excellent ones:

    First Day in School by Bill Binzen (Doubleday, 1972)

    First Day of School by Helen Oxenbury (Dial Books for Young People, 1983)

> *I'd Rather Stay Home* by Carol Buckin
> (Raintree, 1975)
> *School Bus* by Donald Crews (Greenwillow,
> 1984)
> *The Berenstain Bears Go to School* by Stanley
> Berenstain (Random House, 1978).

HOME IDEAS TO HELP MAKE SCHOOL A SUCCESS

The following questionnaire appeared in the December, 1986 issue of *Reader's Digest*. While some of the statements may appear to be geared toward older students, the idea behind the questionnaire is a sound one for parents of all school-age children. The comments that follow each statement are mine.

Score two points for each statement that is "almost always true" of your home; score one point if it's "sometimes true;" score zero if it's "rarely or never true."

1. Everyone in my family has a household responsibility, at least one chore that must be done on time.

It's never too late to begin giving children some responsibility around the house, if you haven't up to this point. If they have not been made accountable for the little things at home, they will have a difficult time assuming responsibility for work at school.

2. We have regular times for members of the family to eat, sleep, play, work, and study.

If your household is characterized by a total lack of organization and structure, then your children will have a difficult time adapting to the expectations of most school environments. See what you can do to get your own life organized and you will find the benefits spill over to your children.

3. Schoolwork and reading come before play, TV, or even other work.

Make sure you build in a regular read-aloud time every evening for your children. Try not to let anything interfere with this time together. They will soon get the message that reading and school responsibilities are important!

4. I praise my child for good schoolwork, sometimes in front of other people.

Don't overdo praise for your children in front of other people, especially when they have children the same age. But praising to Grandma and Grandpa is always acceptable! Display schoolwork on a cork bulletin board or on the refrigerator. Your children will be eager to share their work with you.

5. My child has a quiet place to study, a desk or table at which to work, and books, including a dictionary or other reference material.

Even if you don't have the space or resources for desks for your children, make sure they have a space where they can save their school papers (cardboard files are wonderful for this), a spot to show off their best work (affix to the refrigerator with magnets), a shelf to hold their own books, (board and bricks make good bookshelves), and a table where they can work on projects of their own.

6. Members of my family talk about hobbies, games, news, books we're reading, and movies and TV programs we've seen.

Set aside time at the dinner table each evening to share conversation about the above topics. Don't worry if what you're talking about sometimes seems to go over your children's head. You'll be surprised at how much they're absorbing.

7. The family visits museums, libraries, zoos, historical sites, and other places of interest.

See the lists of Field Trips in Chapters 6, 7, and 8.

8. I encourage good speech habits, helping my child to use the correct words and phrases and to learn new ones.

If your grammar isn't the best or if you have sloppy speech patterns, it's never too late to remediate your speech. It will certainly benefit your children. Encourage them to help you.

9. At dinner, or some other daily occasion, our family talks about the day's events, with a chance for everyone to speak and be listened to.

The old adage "Children should be seen and not heard" is definitely not recommended for parents who want lively, intelligent, inquisitive, and interesting children. Of course, all children need to develop a sense about when it's appropriate to talk or be silent. Good manners never go out of style.

But make sure that you talk about what happened in school every day. In the beginning, you may have to ask many leading questions, but never permit your children to answer the question, "What happened in school today?" with "Nothing."

10. I know my child's current teacher, what my child is doing in school, and which learning materials are being used.

Always learn as much as you can about your children's teachers and curriculum. This information will help you understand what goes on each day at school. You can then encourage and reinforce.

11. I expect quality work and good grades. I know my child's strengths and weaknesses and give encouragement and special help when they're needed.

Never downgrade or make fun of anything your children do in school, no matter how simple or uninspired. Children are most sensitive, and a thoughtless comment can damage a tender ego. Listen to what your children's teachers ask of you and cooperate to the fullest.

12. I talk to my child about the future, about planning for high school and college, and about aiming for a high level of education and vocation.

It's a little early to apply to Harvard, but you can talk about saving money for college and even open a savings account.

If you scored ten or more points, your home ranks in the top one-fourth in terms of the support and encouragement you give your children for school learning. If you scored six or lower, your home is in the bottom one-fourth. If you scored somewhere in-between, you're average in the support you give your children for school learning. Work as a family to bring your score up to ten or more!

In addition to the preceding questionnaire from *The Reader's Digest*, I'd like to add my own set of questions. These have been developed from my years of working with parents as an elementary school principal. I find that the families who can answer "yes" to most of them have children who are successful in school.

1. I'm not afraid to say "no" to my child. I believe that parental discipline is an important prerequisite to "self-discipline."

Children who have never heard the word "no" or learned the difficult lesson of letting someone else have the spotlight have a very difficult time in school. They are so worried about getting their share of the attention, they have little time left for learning.

2. I find out what is happening at school by asking good questions and then carefully listening to what my child is saying about his "school life."

Not every child is willing to share every detail of what happens in school. Many children will respond to parental questions with little, if any, information. But don't give up. Keep asking and then be prepared to listen!

3. I attend all of the conferences, open houses, musical programs, and special events I possibly can.

Being on the scene at school is a perfect way to meet other parents, get to know teachers on a more personal basis, and get a sense of what your child's school is really all about. Even if school wasn't your favorite place to be as a child or young person, put aside your own hesitant feelings and get involved!

4. I model goal-setting and task completion so that my child can see good work habits. I understand that what I do is far more important than anything I say.

You cannot expect your child to finish assignments or start homework without nagging if you keep putting off required tasks or never complete the needlework or remodeling project you started last year. Children need to see that adults overcome procrastination and fear of failure before they are able to do it.

5. I am always willing to learn something new and model being a learner in front of my child.

Get excited about learning a new skill. Sign up for a class at church or community college. Read a book. Talk about a new idea. Demonstrate that learning is a lifelong activity and is NOT limited to school and classrooms.

6. I am willing to admit that I am wrong or have made a mistake and am ready to apologize, even to my own child, for my wrongdoing.

We all admit that we're not perfect (to ourselves and a few close friends). We also need to be ready to admit it to our children. They will be able to pick themselves up after failure and defeat when they see their parents do the same.

7. I encourage my child to talk about his friends, and plan activities and outings that give him an opportunity to make friends and play with them. I make an effort to talk with him about friendships and model the act of making and keeping friends.

The best way to keep track of what's going on in your child's life is to know who his friends are. This process doesn't begin in high school; it begins in nursery school. Invite friends in to play. Meet and talk with other parents. Keep your child involved in an active social life that you can guide and monitor.

8. I support and encourage my child's interests and am willing to let him learn something new or try an unusual hobby or activity from time to time.

There will be times when you don't have the financial resources to sign your child up for another round of music lessons, but give him the benefit of the doubt once in awhile. Children need to experiment with a variety of interests before they find out where their talents and interests lie.

9. I respect my child as an individual and am a good listener when he has problems at school.

You don't need to solve all of the social, emotional, and academic problems that your child may encounter, but you do need to provide a listening ear and a sympathetic attitude when he feels like talking.

10. I respect my child's principal and teachers and let my child know that he should do the same.

Even if you violently disagree with a stand or action taken by a member of the school staff, try not to let those feelings undermine your child's feelings of respect and cooperation for these important adults. School personnel can make mistakes, but you should never give your child an excuse for unacceptable behavior by permitting him to think he doesn't have to follow the rules and meet the standards.

WHAT IF SOMETHING IS WRONG WITH MY CHILD AT SCHOOL?

There are several important principles to remember when dealing with problems in the school setting.

- If your child doesn't talk a great deal about what is happening at school, don't be reluctant to "give him the third degree." Don't accept "nothing" or "fine" as answers to questions. You will need feedback from your child if you are to fully understand a school problem.

- If you feel uncomfortable about something you have seen or heard, contact your child's teacher or the principal. Do your questioning in a calm and reasonable way. You do have a right to ask questions, and you should never overlook anything that troubles you.

- Remember that while you are teaching your child respect for rules and the teachers who have made the rules, you are still an advocate for your child. On some occasions you will need to help your child understand why a teacher has behaved in a certain way or how to cope in a particularly difficult situation.

- If you have a problem and feel that your questions are going unanswered or your concerns are not being addressed, don't be afraid of going to the next level. If you remain calm and reasonable, your efforts will not go unrewarded. Your job is to ensure your child's success in school. Sometimes this means being assertive!

- If you are emotionally invested in a school problem and find it difficult to maintain your objectivity, bring a friend or relative to any school meetings. The presence of a third party can help everyone do a better job of problem solving. You will also gain a different perspective on what happened during the meeting.

WHERE CAN I GO FOR ADDITIONAL INFORMATION?

Here are a few more resources you can consult to make your child's off-to-school experience as smooth as possible:

IS YOUR CHILD IN THE WRONG GRADE? (Louise Bates Ames, Harper & Row, 1967)—A discussion of school readiness and rushing children into structured academics before they are ready.

YOUR CHILD AND THE FIRST YEAR OF SCHOOL (Bernard Ryan, Jr., The World Publishing Co., 1969)—An in-depth look at kindergarten. Although a bit outdated, there is plenty of helpful information. A more recent title by Ryan is *How to Help Your Child Start School* (Soundview Books, 1980).

YOUR CHILD IN SCHOOL: KINDERGARTEN THROUGH SECOND GRADE (Tom and Harriet Sobol, Arbor House, 1987)—A good overview of what to expect in the early elementary grades.

1. Uphoff, J. K. "Age at School Entrance: How Many Are Ready for Success," *Educational Leadership*, Sept. 1985, pp. 86-90).
2. Gilmore, J. E. "How Summer Children Benefit from a Delayed Start in School." Paper presented at the annual conference of the Ohio School Psychologists Association, Cincinnati, May, 1984.
3. Ryan, Bernard, Jr. *How to Help Your Child Start School*, Soundview Books, Darien, Connecticut, 1980, pp. 134-136.

Afterword

IF YOU READ A BOOK THE WAY I OFTEN DO, this might be the first place you've turned! In that case, you have an opportunity to preview the key themes of this book. To those readers who have read this book in a more traditional way, I hope the following will serve to reinforce what you've been reading and thinking about along the way.

- School success is a topic worthy of the attention and understanding of every parent.
- Early learning is a key component of school success.
- The best approach to early learning is one which allows children to develop on their own timetable as we expose them to a wide variety of books, materials, and activities.
- Parents can expose their children to these activities with just a little extra time, effort, and energy.
- Each child has his or her own learning style which affects how information and experiences are processed.
- Attending the right kind of preschool can be a valuable experience.
- Working and single parents face special challenges, but their children, too, can achieve school success. Tap the resources of friends, school, family, the church, and community to share the joys and responsibilities of parenting.
- Every child can learn!

Biblio-
graphy

Bibliography

ALBERT, LINDA, and POPKIN, MICHAEL
  Quality Parenting, New York, Random House, 1987.
AMES, LOUISE BATES
  Don't Push Your Preschooler, New York, Harper & Row, 1980.
  Is Your Child in the Wrong Grade? New York, Harper & Row, 1967.
AMES, LOUISE BATES; GILLESPIES, CLYDE; HAINES, JACQUELINE; and
ILG, FRANCES
  *The Gesell Institute's Child From One to Six: Evaluating the Behavior of the
  Preschool Child,* New York, Harper & Row, 1979.
ANBAR, ADA
  How to Choose a Nursery School: A Parents' Guide to Preschool Education, Palo
  Alto, California, 1982.
ARMSTRONG, THOMAS
  *In Their Own Way: Discovering and Encouraging Your Child's Personal
  Learning Style,* New York, St. Martin's Press, 1987.
ARNOLD, ARNOLD
  Teaching Your Child to Learn from Birth to School Age, Englewood Cliffs, New
  Jersey, Prentice-Hall, Inc., 1971.
ASTON, ATHINA
  Toys That Teach Your Child, Charlotte, North Carolina, East Woods Press, 1984.
AUCKETT, AMELIA D.
  Baby Massage: Parent-Child Bonding Through Touching, New York,
  Newmarket Press, 1981.
AUERBACH, STEVANNE
  The Toy Chest: A Sourcebook of Toys for Children, New York, Lyle Stuart Inc.,
  1986.
BARATTA, MARY LORTON
  Workjobs for Parents, Reading, Massachusetts, Addison-Wesley, 1975.
BASILE, LEONARD J., and CERNAK, ANNE S.
  *The Teacher's Idea Catalog: How to Create Learning Materials for Young
  Children,* Englewood Cliffs, New Jersey, Prentice-Hall, Inc., 1982.
BEADLE, MURIEL
  A Child's Mind, Garden City, New York, Doubleday Co., Inc., 1970.
BECK, JOAN
  Best Beginnings, New York, G.P. Putnam's Sons, 1983.
  How to Raise a Brighter Child, New York, Trident Press, 1967.
BERAM, SANDY
  Games on the Go, New York, Collier Books, 1979.

BLOOM, BENJAMIN
All Our Children Learning, New York, McGraw Hill Book Company, 1981.
Developing Talent in Young People, New York, Ballantine Books, 1985.
Stability and Change in Human Charateristics, New York, John Wiley & Sons, Inc., 1964.
Bloom's Taxonomy of Educational Objectives, Book 1, Cognitive Domain, New York, Longman, 1954.

BOSTON CHILDREN'S MEDICAL CENTER, and GREGG, ELIZABETH M.
What to Do When There's Nothing to Do, New York, Delacorte Press, 1967.

BROWN, DORIS V., and MCDONALD PAULINE
Learning Begins at Home: A Stimulus for a Child's IQ, Los Angeles, California, Lawrence Publishing Co., 1969.

BROWN, SAM
Bubbles, Rainbows & Worms: Science Experiments For Preschool Children, Mt. Rainier, Maryland, Gryphon House, Inc., 1961.

BRUNER, JEROME
Child's Talk: Learning to Use Language, New York, W.W. Norton, 1983.
Studies in Cognitive Growth, New York, John Wiley & Sons, Inc., 1967.

BURTT, KENT GARLAND
Smart Times: A Parents' Guide to Quality Time with Preschoolers, New York, Harper & Row, 1984.

BURTT, KENT GARLAND, and KALKSTEIN, KAREN
Smart Toys for Babies from Birth to Two, New York, Harper & Row, 1981.

BUTLER, DOROTHY, and CLAY, MARIE
Reading Begins at Home, Exeter, New Hampshire, Heinemann Educational Books, Inc., 1979.

CAPLAN, FRANK, and CAPLAN, THERESA
The Power of Play, Garden City, New York, Anchor Press, 1973.

CATALDO, CHRISTINE Z.
Infant and Toddler Programs: A Guide to Very Early Childhood Education, Reading, Massachusetts, Addison-Wesley Publishing Co., 1983.

CHAPPEL, BERNICE M.
A Time for Learning, Ann Arbor, Michigan, Ann Arbor Publishers, 1979.

CHESS, STELLA, and WHITBREAD, JANE
How to Help Your Child Get the Most Out of School, Garden City, New York, Doubleday & Company, Inc., 1974.

CLINE, VICTOR
How to Make Your Child a Winner, New York, Walker & Company, 1980.

COLE, ANN; HAAS, CAROLYN; BUSHNELL, FAITH; and WEINBERGER, BETTY
I Saw a Purple Cow and 100 Other Recipes for Learning, Boston, Little, Brown and Company, 1972.

COLEMAN, JAMES
Report on Educational Opportunity in the United States, Washington, D.C., U.S. Government Printing Office, 1966.

COPPERMAN, PAUL
Taking Books to Heart: Develop a Love of Reading in Your Child, Reading, Massachusetts, Addison-Wesley Publishing Co., 1986.

COPPOLA, RAYMOND T.
Successful Children, New York, Walker & Company, 1978.

DOMAN, GLEN
   How to Multiply Your Baby's Intelligence, New York, Doubleday & Co., 1984.
   How to Teach Your Baby to Read, New York, Random House, 1964.
   Teach Your Baby Math, New York, Simon & Schuster, 1964.

DONALDSON, MARIE
   Children's Minds, New York, W.W. Norton Company, 1978.

DRESKIN, WILLIAM, and DRESKIN, WENDY
   The Daycare Decision, New York, M. Evans & Co., Inc., 1983.

DUNFORD, JILL
   Teach Me Mommy: A Preschool Learning Guide, Cincinnati, Ohio, Writer's
   Digest Books, 1984.

DURKIN, DOLORES
   Children Who Read Early, New York, Teachers College Press, 1966.

EASTMAN, PEGGY, and BARR, JOHN
   Your Child Is Smarter Than You Think, New York, William M. Morrow &
   Co., 1985.

EDELSON, KENNETH, and OREM, R.C.
   Children's House: A Parent/Teacher Guide to Montessori, New York, G.P.
   Putnam's Sons, 1970.

EDSON, LEE
   How We Learn, New York, Time-Life Books, 1975.

ELKIND, DAVID
   The Hurried Child: Growing Up Too Fast, Too Soon, Reading, Massachusetts,
   Addison-Wesley, 1981.
   Miseducation: Preschoolers at Risk, New York, Alfred A. Knopf, 1987.

ENGELMANN, SIEGRID, and ENGELMANN, THERESE
   Give Your Child a Superior Mind, New York, Simon & Schuster, 1966.

EVANS, THOMAS W.
   The School in the Home, New York, Harper & Row, 1973.

FISHER, DOROTHY CANFIELD
   Montessori for Parents, Cambridge, Massachusetts, Robert Bentley, Inc., 1940.

FISHER, JOHN J.
   More Toys to Grow With: Infants and Toddlers, New York, Putnam Publishing
   Group, 1987.

GAMBRELL, LINDA, and WILSON, ROBERT
   28 Ways to Help Your Child Be a Better Reader, Malvern, Pennsylvania,
   Instructo-McGraw Hill, 1977.

GARDNER, HOWARD
   Frames of Mind: The Theory of Multiple Intelligences, New York, Basic Books,
   Inc., Publishers, 1983.

GILLIS, JACK, and FISE, MARY ELLEN R.
   *The Childwise Catalog: A Consumer Guide to Buying the Safest and Best Products
   for Your Children, Newborns Through Age Five,* New York, Pocket Books, 1986.

GOERTZEL, VICTOR, and GOERTZEL, MILDRED G.
   Cradles of Eminence, Boston, Little, Brown and Company, 1962.

GORDON, IRA
   Baby Learning Through Baby Play, New York, St. Martin's Press, 1970.

GORDON, IRA; GUINAGH, BARRY; and JESTER, R. EMILE
Child Learning Through Child Play: Learning Activities for 2 and 3 Year Olds, New York, St. Martin's Press, 1972.

GRAVES, DONALD, and STUART, VIRGINIA
Write from the Start: Tapping Your Child's Natural Writing Ability, New York, E.P. Dutton, 1985.

GREENE, LAWRENCE J.
Learning Disabilities and Your Child: A Survival Handbook, New York, Fawcett Columbine, 1983.

GRILLI, SUSAN
Preschool in the Suzuki Spirit, Tokyo, Japan, Harcourt Brace Jovanovich, 1987.

HAGSTROM, JULIE
Traveling Games for Babies: A Handbook of Games for Infants to Five-Year-Olds, New York, A & W Visual Library, 1981.

HAINSTOCK, ELIZABETH G.
Teaching Montessori in the Home, New York, Random House, 1968.

HANSON, JEANNE K.
Game Plans for Children: Raising a Brighter Child in 10 Minutes a Day, New York, A Perigee Book, 1981.

HEALY, JANE M.
Your Child's Growing Mind: A Parent's Guide to Learning From Birth to Adolescence, Garden City, New York, Doubleday & Company, Inc., 1987.

HECHINGER, FRED M., Editor
A Better Start: New Choices for Early Learning, New York, Walker and Co., 1986.

HIRSCH, C.D.; KETT, JOSEPH F.; and TREFIL, JAMES
Cultural Literacy: What Every American Ought to Know, Boston, Houghton Mifflin, 1987.
The Dictionary of Cultural Literacy, Boston, Houghton Mifflin, 1988.

HUNT, J. McVICKER
Intelligence and Experience, New York, The Ronald Press, 1961.

HUNT, TAMARA, and RENFRO, NANCY
Puppetry in Early Childhood Education, Austin, Texas, Nancy Renfro Studio, 1982.

IBUKA, MASARU
Kindergarten Is Too Late, New York, Simon & Schuster, 1977.

ILG, FRANCES L., and AMES, LOUISE BATES
School Readiness: Behavior Tests Used at the Gesell Institute, New York, Harper & Row Publishers, 1972.

JOHNSON, DORIS McNEELY
Children's Toys and Books: Choosing the Best for All Ages, New York, Charles Scribner's Sons, 1980.

JOHNSON, JUNE
838 Ways to Amuse a Child: Crafts, Hobbies, and Creative Ideas for Children from 6-12, New York, Harper Colophon Books, 1983.

JOHNSON, NANCY
How to Insure Your Child's Success in School, Fresno, California, Mike Murach & Associates, 1983.

JONES, CLAUDIA
Parents Are Teachers, Too, Charlotte, Vermont, Williamson Publishing Co., 1988.

JONES, SANDY
Learning for Little Kids: A Parent Sourcebook for the Years 3 to 8, Boston, Houghton Mifflin Co., 1979.

KABAN, BARBARA
Choosing Toys for Children from Birth to Five, New York, Schocken Books, 1979.

KAYE, PEGGY
Games for Reading: Playful Ways to Help Your Child Read, New York, Pantheon Books, 1984.

KELLY, MARGUERITE, and PARSONS, ELIA
The Mother's Almanac, Garden City, New York, Doubleday & Company, Inc., 1975.

KOHL, MARY ANN F.
Scribble Cookies and Other Independent Creative Art Experiences for Children, Bellingham, Washington, Bright Ring Publications, 1985.

KRANYIK, MARGERY A.
Starting School: How to Help Your Three-to-Eight-Year-Old Make the Most of School, New York, Continuum, 1982.

LAMME, LINDA LEONARD
Growing Up Writing, Washington, D.C., Acropolis Books, 1984.

LEDSON, SIDNEY
Raising Brighter Children, New York, Walker, 1987.

LEDSON, SIDNEY
Teach Your Child to Read in 60 Days, New York, W.W. Norton & Company, Inc., 1975.

LEMBO, JOHN M.
When Learning Happens, New York, Schocken Books, 1972.

LEVENSTEIN, PHYLLIS
Messages from Home: The Mother-Child Home Progam and the Prevention of School Disadvantage, Columbus, Ohio, Ohio State University Press, 1988.

LICKONA, THOMAS
Raising Good Children, New York, Bantam Books, 1983.

LIEPMANN, LISE
Your Child's Sensory World, New York, The Dial Press, 1973.

LYNCH-FRASER, DIANE
Danceplay: Creative Movement for Very Young Children, New York, Walker & Company, 1982.

McDIARMID, NORMA J.; PETERSON, MARIA; and SUTHERLAND, JAMES R.
Living and Learning: Interacting with Your Child from Birth to Three, New York, Harcourt Brace Jovanovich, 1975.

McEWAN, ELAINE K.
How to Raise a Reader, Elgin, Illinois, David C. Cook, 1987.
Superkid? Raising Balanced Children in a Superkid World, Elgin, Illinois, David C. Cook, 1988.

MARZOLLO, JEAN, and LLOYD, JANICE
Learning Through Play, New York, Harper & Row Publishers, 1972.

MARZOLLO, JEAN
Supertot, New York, Harper & Row Publishers, 1977.

MELTON, DAVID
How to Help Your Preschooler Learn...More...Faster...& Better, New York, David McKay Co., 1976.

MILLER, JO ANN, and WEISSMAN, SUSAN
The Parents' Guide to Daycare, New York, Bantam Books, 1986.

MITCHELL, GRACE
The Day Care Book, New York, Stein and Day Publishers, 1979.

MONTESSORI, MARIA
The Absorbent Mind, New York, Holt Rinehart and Winston, 1967.

MOORE, RAYMOND S., and MOORE, DOROTHY N.
Home Grown Kids, Waco, Texas, Word Books, 1981.
Home Style Teaching, Waco, Texas, Word Books, 1984.
School Can Wait, Salt Lake City, Utah, Brigham Young University Press, 1979.

NEWSON, JOHN, and NEWSON, ELIZABETH
Toys and Playthings: In Development and Remediation, New York, Pantheon Books, 1979.

OPPENHEIM, JOANNE
Buy Me, Buy Me, New York, Pantheon Books, 1987.
Kids and Play, New York, Ballantine Books, 1984.

PAGNONI, MARIO
Computers and Small Fries: A Computer Readiness Guide for Parents of Tots, Toddlers, and Other Minors, Wayne, New Jersey, Avery Publishing Group, Inc., 1987.

PAINTER, GENEVIEVE
Teach Your Baby, New York, Simon & Schuster, 1982.

PIAGET, JEAN
The Origins of Intelligence in Children, New York, International Universities Press, 1952.
The Construction of Reality in the Child, New York, Basic Books, 1964.
The Language and Thought of the Child, New York, Basic Books, 1959.

PINCUS, CYNTHIA; ELIOT, LESLIE; and SCHLACHTER, TRUDY
The Roots of Success, New York, Prentice-Hall, Inc., 1978.

PINES, MAYA
Revolution in Learning: The Years from Birth to Six, New York, Harper & Row Publishers, 1967.

PRICE, JANE
How to Have a Child and Keep Your Job, New York, St. Martin's Press, 1979.

PRUDDEN, BONNIE
How to Keep Your Child Fit From Birth to Six, New York, Harper & Row, Publishers, 1964.

PRUDDEN, SUZY
Suzy Prudden's Exercise Program for Young Children 4 Weeks to 4 Years, New York, Workman Publishing, 1983.

RESTAK, RICHARD M.
The Infant Mind, Garden City, New York, Doubleday & Company, Inc., 1986.

RICE, MARY F., and FLATTER, CHARLES H.
Help Me Learn: A Handbook for Teaching Children from Birth to Third Grade, New York, Prentice-Hall, Inc., 1979.

RILEY, SUE SPAYTH
How to Generate Values in Young Children, Los Angeles, California, The New South Company, 1979.

RIMM, SYLVIA
Underachievment Syndrome: Causes and Cures, Watertown, Wisconsin, Apple Publishing Company, 1986.

ROGERS, FRED, and HEAD, BARRY
Mister Rogers' Playbook, New York, Berkley Books, 1986.

RUBIN, RICHARD R., and FISHER, JOHN J.
Your Preschooler, New York, Macmillan, 1982.

RUBIN, RICHARD R.; FISHER, JOHN J.; and DOERING, SUSAN G.
Your Toddler, New York, Macmillan, 1980.

RYAN, BERNARD, JR.
How to Help Your Child Start School, Darien, Connecticut, Soundview Books, 1980.
Your Child and the First Year of School, New York, The World Publishing Company, 1969.

SATIR, VIRGINIA
Peoplemaking, Palo Alto, California, Science and Behavior Books, Inc., 1972.

SAUNDERS, JACQULYN, and ESPELAND, PAMELA
Bringing Out the Best, Minneapolis, Minnesota, Free Spirit Publishing Co., 1986.

SCHARLATT, ELISABETH, Editor
Kids Day In and Day Out: A Parents' Manual, New York, Simon & Schuster, 1979.

SCHULMAN, MICHAEL, and MEKLER, EVA
Bringing Up a Moral Child, Reading, Massachusetts, Addison-Wesley Publishing Company, 1985.

SEGAL, MARILYN, and ADCOCK, DON
Your Child at Play: One to Two Years Exploring, Daily Living, Learning and Making Friends, New York, Newmarket Press, 1985.

SHARP, EVELYN
Thinking Is Child's Play, New York, Avon Books, 1969.

SHERIDAN, MARY D.
Spontaneous Play in Early Childhood: From Birth to Six Years, Berks, England, NFER Publishing Co., 1977.

SHIFF, EILEEN, Editor
Experts Advise Parents, New York, Delacorte, 1987.

SIEGEL-GORELICK, BRYNA
The Working Parents' Guide to Child Care, Boston, Little, Brown and Company, 1983.

SIME, MARY
A Child's Eye View: Piaget for Young Parents and Teachers, New York, Harper & Row Publishers, 1973.

SINGER, DOROTHY G., and SINGER, JEROME L.
Partners in Play: A Step-By Step Guide to Imaginative Play, New York, Harper & Row Publishers, 1977.

SMETHURST, WOOD
Teaching Young Children to Read at Home, New York, McGraw Hill Book Co., 1975.

SMITH, HELEN WHEELER
Survival Handbook for Preschool Mothers, Chicago, Follett Publishing Co., 1977.

SOBOL, TOM and HARRIET
Your Child in School: Kindergarten through Second Grade, New York, Arbor House, 1987.

SPARKMAN, BRANDON, and CARMICHAEL, BRANDON
Blueprint for a Brighter Child, New York, McGraw-Hill Book Company, 1973.

SPARLING, JOSEPH, and LEWIS, ISABELLE
Learning Games for Threes and Fours: A Guide to Adult-Child Play, New York, Walker and Company, 1984.

SPENCER, MARY ANN PULASKI
Your Baby's Mind and How It Grows: Piaget's Theory for Parents, New York, Harper & Row, 1978.

SPRINGER, SALLY P., and DEUTSCH, GEORG
Left Brain, Right Brain, San Francisco, California, W.H. Freeman and Company, 1981.

STEIN, SARA BONNETT
Learn at Home the Sesame Street Way, New York, Simon & Schuster, 1979.

STERNBERG, ROBERT
Beyond IQ: A Triarchic Theory of Human Intelligence, Cambridge University Press, 1984.

STOCK, CLAUDETTE, and McCLURE, JUDITH S.
The Household Curriculum: A Workbook for Teaching Your Young Child to Think, New York, Harper & Row Publishers, 1983.

STRIKER, SUSAN
Please Touch: How to Stimulate Your Child's Creative Development, New York, Simon & Schuster, Inc., 1986.

SULLIVAN, S. ADAMS
The Quality Time Almanac: A Sourcebook of Ideas and Activities for Parents and Kids, Garden City, New York, Doubleday & Company, 1986.

SUTTON-SMITH, BRIAN, and SUTTON-SMITH, SHIRLEY
How to Play with Your Children, New York, Hawthorn Books, 1974.

TAETZSCH, SANDRA ZEITLIN, and TAETZSCH, LYN
Pre-school Games and Activities, Belmont, California, Pitman Learning, Inc., 1974.

TIME-LIFE BOOKS EDITORS
When Others Care for Your Child, Alexandria, Virginia, Time-Life Books, Inc., 1987.

TOOLE, AMY L., and BOEHM, ELLEN
Off to a Good Start: 464 Readiness Activities for Reading, Math, Social Studies, and Science, New York, Walker & Company, 1983.

ULENE, ART, and SHELOV, STEVEN
Bringing Out the Best in Your Baby, New York, Macmillan, 1986.

VAIL, PRISCILLA L.
Smart Kids with School Problems, New York, E.P. Dutton, 1987.

VAN RIPER, CHARLES GAGE
Teaching Your Child to Talk, New York, Harper & Row, 1950.

VITALE, BARBARA MEISTER
Unicorns Are Real: A Right Brained Approach to Learning, Rolling Hills Estates, CA, Jalmar Press, 1982.

VYGOTSKY, LEV
Thought and Language Cambridge, Massachusetts, The M.I.T. Press, 1962.

WADE, THEODORE E.
The Home School Manual, Auburn, CA, Gazelle Publications, 1984.

WANN, KENNETH D.
Fostering Intellectual Development in Children, New York, Teachers College Press, 1962.

WARREN, VIRGINIA BURGESS
Tested Ways to Help Your Child Learn, Englewood Cliffs, New Jersey, Prentice-Hall, Inc., 1961.

WEBB, JAMES T.; MECKSTROTH, ELIZABETH A.; and TOLAN, STEPHANIE S.
Guiding the Gifted Child: A Practical Source for Parents and Teachers, Columbus, Ohio, Ohio Psychology Publishing Company, 1982.

WEISS, HELEN GINANDES, and WEISS, MARTIN
Home is a Learning Place: A Parents' Guide to Learning Disabilities, Boston, Little Brown and Company, 1976.

WHITE, BURTON L., et. al.
Experience and Environment: Major Influences on the Development of the Young Child, Volume II, Englewood Cliffs, New Jersey, Prentice-Hall, Inc., 1978.

WHITE, BURTON L.
A Parent's Guide to the First Three Years, Englewood Cliffs, New Jersey, Prentice-Hall, Inc., 1980.
The First Three Years of Life, Englewood Cliffs, New Jersey, Prentice-Hall, Inc., 1975.
The Origins of Human Competence: The Final Report of the Harvard Preschool Project, Lexington, Massachusetts, Lexington Books, 1979.

WIENER, HARVEY S.
Talk with Your Child, New York, Viking, 1988.

WILLIAMS, EMILY NEEDHAM
High Tech Babies: An Owner's Manual, Dallas, Texas, Presswords, 1986.

WINNICK, MARIANN P.
Before the 3 R's, New York, David McKay Company, Inc., 1973.

WOLFGANG, MARY E., and MULLE, CORINNE
I'm Ready to Learn: Activities for Preschool and Kindergarten Children, Malvern, Pennsylvania, Instructo-McGraw Hill, 1983.

WOLPER, SHEILA, and LEVINE, BETH
Playgroups, New York, Pocket Books, 1988.

ZASLAVSKY, CLAUDIA
Preparing Young Children for Math: A Book of Games, New York, Schocken, 1979.